Ace Your Life

Ace Your Life

Life Management Skills Made Easy

Michele Sfakianos, RN, BSN

Open Pages Publishing, LLC
Fort Myers, FL 33906

Ace Your Life: Life Management Skills Made Easy
© 2014 Michele Sfakianos, RN, BSN - All rights reserved.

Open Pages Publishing, LLC
P.O. Box 61048
Fort Myers, FL 33906
http://www.my411books.com/contact/open-pages-publishing
(239) 454–7700

ISBN: (e) 978-0-9960687-1-0
ISBN: (sc) 978-0-9960687-0-3

Library of Congress Control Number: 2014909101

Printed in the United States of America
Because of the dynamic nature of the Internet, any Web addresses or links contained in this book may have changed since publication and may no longer be valid. The views expressed in this work are solely those of the author and do not necessarily reflect the views of the publisher, and the publisher hereby disclaims any responsibility for them.

Author/Book website: http://www.my411books.com

Disclaimer
The information in this book is:
- of a general nature and not intended to address the specific circumstances of any particular individual or entity;
- written as a guide and is not intended to be a comprehensive tool, but is complete, accurate, or up to date at the time of writing;
- an information tool only and not intended to be used in place of a visit, consultation, or advice of a medical professional;

This book is not intended to serve as professional or legal advice (if you need specific advice, you should always consult a suitably qualified professional).

Table of Contents

Dedication

*This book is dedicated to you, the reader,
and I thank you for taking the time to read and
understand the value of the contents.*

Acknowledgments

Thank you to Mark B. Rudolph, Financial Advisor, for his contribution on the chapter entitled "Money Management." He was of particular assistance with the "Investing" section.

Thank you also to my family for their love and support through this crazy process. I hope that the late nights and weekends dedicated to the writing and research were well worth their sacrifice.

Most of all, I would like to say a big "thank you" to those that supported the first version of this book, *The 4–1–1 on Life Skills*. Without their thirst for information and their incredible faith in me, I would not have been challenged to write a revised edition. I know the hours of internet research and fact checking will help to enlighten the lives of others.

Preface

For years, I have been concerned that there is no type of instruction given on many of the topics in this book. So I decided to do something about it. In my generation (1970s), we took a home economics course in middle school to learn the basics of cooking and sewing. To my knowledge, this course has either been removed or made optional in the current school curriculum. I think it is a shame that this vital information is no longer required. My children were not offered this course at the school they attended.

As a parent, I feel that a basic money management and a home economics course should be required. Our children need to learn how to balance a checkbook, understand depreciation, and be able to maintain a healthy and happy home. Many young adults today do not understand depreciation. They also may not understand how certain items increase in value over the years, so it is imperative to care for these items.

There is also a need to know about 401Ks, 403Bs, and income tax retirement accounts. I didn't have this information until the age of thirty. Saving for retirement is something that should begin with your first job.

You are probably thinking that it is the parents' responsibility to teach all of this to their kids. However, there are many people who were not given this information in their younger years. It is unfortunate that many parents do not know this information to pass on to their children. If they are not learning it at home, then where will they get this information?

It is my hope that this book will help those who need it and will be shared with others who can benefit from it. This is not a "be all, end all" book and it is not intended to replace knowledge received from trained professionals. I want to be able to take some of the burden off the next generation to allow them to focus on the important things in life. As a Registered Nurse and Leading Authority on Life Skills, I want to help the young adults of today and the next generation.

The information contained in this book can be found on the Internet and in single subject matter books. However, I wanted to try to pull everything together into one book for easy reference. Enjoy!

Introduction

Did you ever wonder when you were getting ready to leave home for the first time, if your parents had taught you everything you needed to know to survive on your own? Did you know how to do laundry; clean a home; balance a checkbook or cook a meal? Were you aware of the different types of deposits required to either rent or buy a home? If the answers were "yes" – good for the role models that you had. Thank them every chance you get! If the answers were "no" to most of these questions – look no more – the answers are here for you.

Until you are confronted with taking care of yourself and a home, many people do not realize what is involved. It can be overwhelming to some and totally frustrating to others. Life is meant to be enjoyed. If you equip yourself with the knowledge to take care of the everyday tasks, you will then be able to enjoy other activities.

Whether you are moving out for the first time; or going it alone due to divorce or death of a loved one; or starting a family of your own, this information is for you. The chapters ahead will provide a new dimension of potential for you and your family.

Through the information contained in the following chapters, you will experience the age old, tried and true methods, the strategies that will keep you focused and on target. You will not only benefit from the rewards of your hard work, but your children will also benefit as they grow knowing they will be "prepared" someday too.

I've put all the cards on the table for you. *Ace Your Life*, is the "Ace in the hole" that will provide the tools and knowledge, to gain *that* something, to put you and your family on the pathway of an informed and powerful life.

Chapter 1

Cleaning Supplies:
A Basic List

You do not have to have expensive cleaning supplies to do a good job. Many cleaners have several uses, so check labels to see if you can utilize the product for different types of cleaning. Do not use more than one product at a time. Products can contain harmful chemicals that when mixed could be fatal. Use gloves when cleaning with strong chemicals because your skin will absorb the chemicals. Try to purchase supplies that can be machine washed instead of thrown away after each use, such as removable dusters, mops, and cleaning rags.

Dusting Supplies:
- Cleaning cloths (machine washable)
- Dust mop or vacuum cleaner dusting attachment
- Dusting spray and/or furniture polish (Hint: dryer sheets work well for dusting.)

General Surface Supplies: (Use "green" supplies to help save our environment)
- Kitchen cleaner or wipes
- All-purpose cleaner
- Vinegar
- Bathroom cleaner or wipes
- Mildew remover
- Scrubbers
- Gloves

Special Area Cleaners:

- Automatic dishwasher detergent
- Oven cleaner
- Cleaner for glass top stove
- Dish soap
- Wood polish (works well on wood cabinets)
- Upholstery spot remover
- Carpet cleaner
- Carpet spot remover
- Leather cleaner
- Laundry soap
- Laundry stain remover
- Toilet bowl cleaners
- Soft scrubbing cleanser (preferably with bleach)
- Air freshener (look for antibacterial)
- Glass cleaner

Floor Cleaning Supplies:

- Broom
- Dustpan
- Vacuum cleaner
- Mop (replace often or wash if machine washable)
- Mop bucket
- Mopping solution (¼ cup vinegar and a bucket of water works well). Optional: Floor Steamer – delivers a hot steam that helps to remove dirt from floor areas.

Chapter 2

Cleaning Your Home

You do not have to have a "white-glove" home. This chapter is intended to serve as a guide for a clean home. Take good care of your home, both inside and out, so that it will last for a long time. General everyday pick up of items is always recommended. You never know who will stop by. It may seem like a lot, but once you get into the swing of things, it will take you less time to clean. You will find some redundant items in each section, but each room needs to have these items completed. I have found that if it isn't in writing, it may not get done.

There is a difference between organizing, cleaning and disinfecting (sanitizing). Organizing is finding a place for everything. Cleaning is removing the dirt, dust and grime. Disinfecting is the process of removing the bacteria and germs (also known as "microbes") to a safe level in your home.

Make sure to check the dwell times on each cleaner. This is the amount of time that the cleaner needs to sit after application before you wipe it off. Make sure to apply spray cleaners directly to a cloth and wipe the surface. Spraying cleaners into the air can cause respiratory irritation, especially for those with asthma or allergy symptoms. If you are going on a trip, make sure to clean your house before you leave. You will feel so much better returning to a clean home. Think about how tired you get on vacation. Coming home to a mess is stressful. This is not something taught in school. I had to learn over the years what worked best for me, and I am passing this information on to you. Create your own style with the suggestions below.

Bathroom:
- Keep the toilet paper roll filled. Keep extra rolls in the cabinet nearest to the toilet.
- Keep a room freshener close by the commode.
- Clean sink and wipe down sink area once a week.
- Wipe down any decorations, toothbrush holders, mirror, etc. once a week.
- Clean toilet: wipe down the toilet seat (top and bottom), toilet cover, and toilet top rim once a week.
- Clean tub/shower: move all items out of shower before cleaning once a week.
- Wipe down windowsills with damp cloth once a week.
- Sweep/mop floor once a week.
- Wipe baseboards with a damp cloth every three months.
- Wash hand towels at least once a week or more if soiled.
- Keep floor mats flat to prevent tripping.
- Wash floor mats every three months.
- Use a plastic liner with your shower curtain. Keep the shower curtain closed (stretched from side to side) to help prevent mildew on the liner. If it does mildew, wash the liner in the washing machine and hang to dry back in the shower. Or just replace the liner. You can find an inexpensive liner in a local discount store.

Bedrooms (Master, Guest and Child):
- Keep items off the floor.
- Wash pillows, duvets, mattress covers, and comforters every three months.
- Wipe ceiling fans with damp cloth once a month.
- Wipe baseboards with a damp cloth every three months.
- Dust once a week: move all items off shelves and wipe clean before putting back.
- Sweep/vacuum floor once a week.

- Change sheets once a week or no longer than two weeks. (or after Guests)
- Use a clean upholstery attachment and vacuum your mattress when you change your sheets. The average mattress has any where from 10,000 to 10,000,000 dust mites.
- Dust blinds and wipe windowsills with damp cloth once a month.
- Keep blind pulls out of reach of children.
- Wash curtains (if machine washable) every three months.
- Mop/steam tile floors once a week.
- Use a damp cloth mop (not soaking) for wood floors. You can also use a floor steamer on wood floors. Do not allow water to sit on wood floors (especially laminate wood floors.)
- Keep toys in bins when not in use. (child room)
- Have a waterproof mattress pad on the bed for young children.

Living Room/Family Room:
- Keep picked up daily.
- Keep remote controls together in one place.
- Wipe ceiling fans with damp cloth once a month.
- Dust blinds and wipe windowsills with damp cloth once a month.
- Keep blind pulls out of reach of children.
- Wash curtains (if machine washable) every three months.
- Wipe baseboards with a damp cloth every three months.
- Dust once a week: move all items off shelves and wipe clean before putting back.
- Sweep/vacuum floor/carpet once a week.
- Mop/steam tile floors once a week.
- Use a damp cloth mop (not soaking) for wood floors. You can also use a floor steamer on wood floors. Do not allow water to sit on wood floors (especially laminate wood floors.)

Kitchen/Dining Area:
- Load dishwasher instead of stacking dishes in sink. Scrape food bits off before loading to reduce particles stuck on dishes once the cycle is over.

- If you don't have a dishwasher, rinse dishes well after use then stack in sink.
- Wash dishes every night in warm/hot soapy water. Don't leave dishes sitting in the sink until the morning. Do not just put some soap on a cloth to wash the dishes. Instead, fill the sink with hot soapy water and allow the dishes to soak while you wash.
- Run dishwasher when full. Do not overcrowd the dishwasher It is best to wash a few dishes by hand than to have to rerun the dishwasher because the dishes were too close together. No small loads—conserve water.
- Keep countertops wiped down.
- Wash hand towels and dish cloths at least once a week or more if soiled.
- Toss sponges in the dishwasher weekly to clean.
- Pick up food off floor immediately when spilled.
- Wipe baseboards with a damp cloth every three months.
- Take trash out when full and replace bag. Clean the trash container if soiled before replacing the bag.
- Wipe stove area nightly (and when soiled).
- Wipe out the microwave after each use. For difficult to clean splatters, take a half of a lemon and put it in a small bowl filled half way with water into the microwave on high power for 3-5 minutes, then wipe clean.
- Wipe glass stove tops nightly (and when soiled). Use water and a soft rag to avoid scratches or a special cleaner designed for glass tops only.
- Keep pantry/shelves clutter-free.
- Sweep floor nightly.
- Mop/steam once a week or more for spills.
- Wash curtains (if machine washable) every three months.
- Use a damp cloth mop (not soaking) for wood floors. You can also use a floor steamer on wood floors. Do not allow water to sit on wood floors (especially laminate wood floors.)
- Wipe cabinets down every three months with a damp cloth. Furniture oil works well. Never use harsh chemicals.

- Keep kitchen table cleared.
- Wipe down kitchen table after each meal.
- If you spill something in the oven, once it has cooled, wipe it out. This will prevent that burnt smell when cooking in the oven next time.
- Run an empty dishwasher with vinegar. It's the same concept as running a vinegar load in your washing machine. You simply pour a cup of white vinegar into the bottom of an empty dishwasher once a month and run a normal cycle. It cleans out old food particles to keep your dishwasher smelling fresh.

Refrigerator Cleaning:

- Keep refrigerator door handle wiped clean.
- Wipe refrigerator shelves and walls with a damp cloth once a month.
- For Stainless Steel Refrigerator – use manufacturer recommended cleaner.
- If food has spoiled in a refrigerator – such as during a power outage – and odors from the food remain, they can be difficult to remove. The following procedures may have to be repeated.
  - Wipe inside of unit with equal parts vinegar and water. Vinegar provides acid which destroys mildew.
  - Wash inside of unit with a solution of baking soda and water. Be sure to scrub the gaskets, shelves, sides, and door. Allow to air out several days.
  - Fill unit with rolled newspapers. Close the door and leave for several days. Remove paper and clean with vinegar and water.
  - Sprinkle fresh coffee grounds or baking soda loosely in the bottom of the unit, or place them in an open container.
  - Place a cotton swab soaked with vanilla inside freezer. Close door for 24 hours. Check for odors.
  - Use a commercial product available at hardware and housewares stores. Follow the manufacturers' instructions.

Closets:
- Keep floors free of clutter.
- Stack items on shelves carefully—do not over stack.
- For linen closets, stack towels, washcloths, hand towels and bed sheets in separate piles.

Furniture:
- Vacuum furniture (inside and out) monthly, especially if you have a pet.
- For leather furniture, follow the manufacturer's instructions.
- Spot treat stains immediately.

Area Rugs:
- Rugs take up a large portion of square footage in our living rooms and can be the focal point that pulls an entire room together. They also get some serious foot traffic. This is why it's important to maintain a regular cleaning schedule. If they become a source of dirt and dust buildup, this can lead to allergies.
- Vacuum every two weeks or sooner for heavy traffic.
- Immediately spot clean any spills.
- Rugs fade with too much sunlight so rotate every six months.
- Once a year, treat your rug to a deep steam cleaning to remove embedded dirt and dust buildup. This will improve the overall appearance and longevity.

Electronics and Appliances:
- Dust once a week (TV, electronic games, stereo, computer, etc) with a microfiber cloth or an electrostatic duster.
- Wipe phones with a damp cloth once a week or more if someone is sick. When you or someone in the home is sick, spray the cloth with an antimicrobial cleaner before cleaning.
- Clean vacuum attachments by washing with soapy water every three months or sooner if needed.

Misc. Filters:
- Change sink water filters as directed by manufacturer.

- Check to see if your refrigerator has a water filter and change it every six months.
- Change the filter in your vacuum cleaner often to extend the life of the product and minimize allergy-related problems. Make sure to empty your vacuum bag or container and wash it out if it's made of hard plastic. Wash the sponge-type filters often to prevent from having to purchase new ones.

Batteries:
- Change smoke alarm batteries once a year (or sooner if they chirp). Some people like to change every six months. January 1 is a good reference date (New Year = New Batteries).

Air Conditioner/Heater/Furnace/Fireplace:
- Change air conditioner filters once a month. Dust and Dust mites are one of the major contributors of allergies and allergic reactions.
- Have your air conditioner and/or furnace serviced once a year.
- Clean your furnace every 4–6 months to extend the life and prevent costly repairs. A dirty furnace will burn higher amounts of electric and gas fuel, as well as work less effectively than a clean furnace. There are 3 basic parts of your furnace that can be impacted by the presence of dirt: the filter system, the blower, and the motor.
- Replace furnace filters on air driven systems once a month during heating season.
- Vacuum vents to remove dust and dirt so that dirt does not further tax your heating or cooling system.
- Clean your fireplace/chimney once a year during the summer months or sooner if used often. If you are not comfortable cleaning the fireplace/chimney, hire a professional.

Light Bulbs:
- Change light bulbs when they burn out. Do not remove a light bulb and leave the socket empty. It is a known fact that you can be electrocuted by sticking your finger in an empty light socket.

- To conserve energy, do not use a bulb with a wattage higher than 60.

Windows:
- Clean all your windows (inside and out) at least every six months.
- Clean sliding glass doors at least once a week.
- Keep your windows locked (if you have a lock). If you don't have locks and have windows that lift up and down, place a wooden stick to jar the window closed so you don't have intruders.

Picture Frames/Wall Coverings:
- Whether hanging on the wall or sitting on a table, wipe clean with a damp cloth every two weeks.
- Dust wall coverings every two weeks.

Doors:
- Spray and wipe all doors/handle areas with a cleaner once a week or sooner if needed.

Patios:
- Wipe ceiling fans with damp cloth once a month.
- Wipe patio table with a damp cloth once a week.
- Keep area clutter-free.
- Keep toys picked up and in one area.
- Keep a large bin for gardening tools, patio supplies, etc.
- Clean up spills to prevent bugs and pests.

Stairs (if applicable):
- Keep stairs clutter-free.
- Vacuum/sweep once a week.
- Wipe hand rails with damp cloth once a week or sooner if soiled.

Cobwebs:
- Clean the webs from the ceiling/wall areas of each room once a month.

- Clean the webs from light fixtures once a month.
- Clean the webs from patio areas once a month.
- Clean the webs from the garage/carport once a month.

Garage/Carport:
- Organize and keep things in their place.
- Sweep the floor area once a month.
- Apply oil dry to oil spills when they happen to absorb them (may substitute sawdust or kitty litter).
- Keep cleaners, gasoline cans, spray paint cans and any other poisonous liquids out of reach of children.
- Keep tools in one place and out of reach of children.

Smoking:
There is whole other set of cleaning rules for smokers.
- Smoking increases the amount of dust and odors in a home. If you see the dust building up on furniture, then you may need to dust more often than weekly.
- Smoke gets into fabrics (drapes, curtains, clothes, etc.) and upholstered furniture and makes it difficult to get rid of the smell. Most carpet cleaning services offer upholstering cleaning. Make sure to wash window coverings often.
- Smoking in the home makes walls sticky and discolored. If you do not wash the walls frequently, then you will need to repaint more often. You can test this by removing pictures from the walls to see if there is discoloration around them.
- Non-smoking guests may be offended by the smoking odor in your home. If you smoke in the home, try to limit it to one or two rooms that are closed off from where you sit with your guests. Use an ionic air purifier to remove the odor.

Pets:
If you have pets in the home, then you have yet another set of dirt and odors to eliminate.
- Cats can shed fur on sofas, floors and beds. Make sure to vacuum often.

- Kitty litter must be changed regularly to avoid those odors.
- Dogs track in dirt, leave their nose prints, and most times shed their hair all over the home. While outside, they find something dead to roll in and then bring that odor in the home. Make sure to remove these odors promptly.
- Birds scatter their feathers and those seed hulls everywhere but in their cage. Keep a sweeper or vacuum close by.
- Other animals can send additional odors into the air as well. Just because you have become immune to the smell, your guests may not be.

Chapter 3

Kitchen/Grilling Safety and Cooking Basics

Kitchen safety is one of the most important things you need to focus on. Fires can start easily and get out of hand within minutes. The leading cause of fires in the kitchen is unattended cooking. Stay in the kitchen when you are frying, grilling, or broiling food. If you leave the kitchen for even a short period of time, turn off the stove. If you are simmering, baking, roasting, or boiling food, check it regularly. Remain in the home while food is cooking, and use a timer to remind you that you are cooking. If you are using a slow cooker, it is still recommended that you stay home while cooking. To prevent cooking fires, you have to be alert. You will not be alert if you are sleepy; have been drinking alcohol; or have taken medicine that causes drowsiness.

Kitchen Safety:
- Never cook in loose clothes and keep your hair tied back.
- Keep your knives in a wooden block or in a drawer. Keep knives away from children.
- Keep your potholders in the drawer next to the stove.
- Turn pot handles away from the front of the stove. Children can pull on the handle and spill the hot contents on their face or body.
- Wipe spills immediately to avoid anyone slipping and falling on the floor.
- Make sure to separate raw meat and poultry from other items whenever you use or store them.

- Do not use the same cutting board for meat and vegetables without washing between usages.
- Wash your hands before handling food and after handling raw meat and poultry.
- Always use cooking equipment tested and approved by a recognized testing facility.
- Follow manufacturer instructions and code requirements when installing and operating cooking equipment.
- Plug microwave ovens and other cooking appliances directly into an outlet.
- Never use an extension cord for a cooking appliance. It can overload the circuit and cause a fire.
- If your clothes catch fire, stop, drop, and roll. Stop immediately, drop to the ground, and cover your face with your hands. Roll over and over or back and forth to put out the fire. Immediately treat the burn with cool water for three to five minutes and then seek emergency medical care.

Kitchen Fire Safety:

- Keep a larger ABC rated fire extinguisher in the kitchen (check expiration date and pressure gauge periodically). Hang this where you can access it.
- When in doubt, just get out. When you leave, close the door behind you to help contain the fire. Call 911 or the local emergency number after you leave.
- If you try to extinguish the fire, be sure others are getting out and you have a clear path to the exit.
- Always keep an oven mitt and a lid nearby when you are cooking. If a small grease fire starts in a pan, put on the mitt then smother the flames by carefully sliding the lid over the pan. Turn off the burner. Do not move the pan. To keep the fire from restarting, leave the lid on until the pan is completely cool.
- In case of an oven fire, turn off the heat and keep the door closed to prevent flames from burning you or your clothing.
- If you have a fire in your microwave oven, turn it off immediately and keep the door closed. Never open the door until the fire is

completely out. Unplug the appliance if you can safely reach the outlet. Do not stand directly in front of the door.

- After a fire, both ovens and microwaves should be checked and/ or serviced before being used again.

Protect Children from Scalds and Burns:

- Young children are at high risk for being burned by hot food and liquids. Keep children away from cooking areas by enforcing a "kid-free zone" of three feet around the stove.
- Keep young children at least three feet away from any place where hot food or drink is being prepared or carried.
- Keep hot foods and liquids away from table and counter edges.
- When young children are present, use the stove's back burners whenever possible.
- Never hold a child while cooking, drinking, or carrying hot foods or liquids.
- Teach children that hot things burn.
- When children are old enough, teach them to cook safely. Supervise them closely.

Preventing Scalds and Burns:

- To prevent spills due to overturned pots/pans containing hot food or liquids, use the back burner when possible and/or turn pot handles away from the stove's edge. All appliance cords need to be kept coiled and away from counter edges.
- Use oven mitts or potholders when removing hot food from ovens, microwave ovens, or stove tops. Never use wet oven mitts or potholders, as they can cause scald burns.
- Replace old or worn oven mitts.
- Treat a burn right away by putting it in cool water. Cool the burn for three to five minutes. Use a burn cream. If the burn is bigger than your fist or if you have any questions about how to treat it, seek medical attention right away.

Install and Use Microwave Ovens Safely:

- Place or install the microwave oven at a safe height, within easy reach of all users. The face of the person using the microwave oven should always be higher than the front of the microwave oven door. This will prevent hot food or liquid from spilling onto a user's face or body from above. It will also prevent the microwave oven itself from falling onto a user.

- Never use aluminum foil or metal objects in a microwave oven. They can cause a fire and damage the oven.
- Heat food only in containers or dishes that are safe for microwave use (glass dishes are preferable).
- Open heated food containers slowly away from the face to avoid steam burns. The hot steam escaping from the container or food can cause burns.
- Foods heat unevenly in microwave ovens. Stir and test before eating.

Smoke Alarms:

- Move smoke alarms farther away from kitchens according to manufacturer instructions and/or install a smoke alarm with a pause button.
- If a smoke alarm sounds during normal cooking, press the pause button if it has one. Open the door or window or fan the area with a towel to get the air moving. Do not disable the smoke alarm or take out the batteries.
- You should treat every smoke alarm that is activated as a likely fire and react quickly and safely to the alarm.

Cooking/Clean Up Basics:

- Clean as you go when cooking a meal. There will be less to clean up afterwards.
- If you burn something in a pan, soak the pan in hot soapy water for only twenty minutes then wash. Do not soak the pan overnight. It will not be any easier to clean.
- Never pour hot grease down the sink. It will cool and harden and clog the drain.
- Do not cook everything on high. If you are following the directions of a recipe, make sure to utilize the temperatures specified. Otherwise, medium to medium-high works best. Turn to low or warm setting until ready to serve.

- Start out with simple recipes with few ingredients that are easy to follow. Once you are comfortable with those, try recipes with a longer list of ingredients.
- If your first meal is not the best, that's okay. Do not give up. You can do it!
- It is best to keep a lid on pots/pans unless otherwise specified. It keeps the heat in and cooks the food quicker.

A meat thermometer is a thermometer used to measure the internal temperature of meat and other cooked foods. The degree of "doneness" of meat correlates closely with the internal temperature, so that a thermometer reading indicates when it is cooked as desired. Meat should always be cooked so that the interior reaches a temperature sufficient to kill pathogens that may cause foodborne illness; the thermometer helps to ensure this.

Temperature Chart: (Temperatures are the internal meat temperature after cooking)

Food Item	Safe Temperature Range (°F)
Ground beef, pork, veal, lamb	160
Ground turkey, chicken	165
Fresh Beef, veal, lamb	145-170
Chicken and turkey, whole	180
Poultry breasts, roasted	170
Poultry thighs, wings	180
Duck and goose	180
Stuffing (cooked alone or in a bird)	165
Fresh pork	160-170
Fresh ham	160
Pre-cooked ham (reheated)	140
Eggs	Cook until yoke and white are firm
Egg dishes	160
Leftovers and casseroles	165

Stove Temperatures:

450–500°F: high

375–400°F: medium–high

325–350°F: medium
275–300°F: medium–low
225–250°F: low

Common Cooking Conversions and Equivalents

Liquid volume equivalents

1 cup = 8 fluid ounces or 16 tablespoons
2 cups = 1 pint or 16 fluid ounces
2 pints = 1 quart or 32 fluid ounces
4 quarts = 1 gallon
½tablespoon = 1½teaspoons
1 tablespoon = 3 teaspoons
2 tablespoons = 1 fluid ounce

Dry equivalents

¼cup = 4 tablespoons
1/3 cup = 5 tablespoons plus 1 teaspoon
½cup = 8 tablespoons or roughly 4 ounces
¾cup = 12 tablespoons
1 cup = 16 tablespoons
1 dry pint = 2 cups or ¾dry quart
1 dry quart = 4 cups or 2 dry pints
1 bushel = 32 dry quarts
1 pound = 16 ounces

Baking equivalents

1 cup sifted cake flour = 1 cup minus 2 tablespoons sifted all-purpose flour
1 cup sifted all-purpose flour = 1 cup plus 2 tablespoons sifted cake flour
1 teaspoon double-acting baking powder = ¼ teaspoon baking soda plus ½ teaspoon cream of tartar

Miscellaneous equivalents

1 tablespoon prepared mustard = 1 teaspoon dried mustard
1 cup stock or broth = 1 bouillon cube dissolved in 1 cup boiling water

1 square (1 ounce) baking unsweetened chocolate = 3 tablespoons cocoa powder plus 1 tablespoon butter

1 ounce semi-sweet chocolate = 3 tablespoons cocoa powder plus 2 tablespoons butter plus 3 tablespoons sugar

Food equivalents

2 slices bread = 1 cup fresh bread crumbs

1 stick butter = 8 tablespoons butter

1 pound butter = 4 sticks butter

1 pound confectioners' sugar = about 4½ cups confectioners' sugar, sifted

1 pound granulated sugar = 2 cups granulated sugar

½ pound hard cheese = about 2 cups grated cheese

1 cup heavy whipping cream = 2 cups whipped cream

1 medium lemon = about 3 tablespoons lemon juice or 2 to 3 teaspoons grated peel

1 pound apples = about 3 apples

1 large onion = about 1 cup chopped onion

1 cup raw converted rice = 3 cups cooked rice

1 large tomato = about ¾ cup chopped tomato

1 pound all-purpose flour = about 4 cups sifted flour

1 stick butter = ½ cup or 4 ounces

Barbecue Grill Safety:

- Position the grill well away from siding, deck railings, and out from under eaves and overhanging branches.
- Place the grill a safe distance from lawn games, play areas, and foot traffic.
- Keep children and pets away from the grill area by declaring a three-foot "kid-free zone."
- Put out several long-handled grilling tools to give the chef plenty of clearance from heat and flames when cooking food.
- Periodically remove grease or fat buildup in trays below grill so it cannot be ignited by a hot grill.
- Use only outdoors. If used indoors, or in any enclosed spaces such as tents, barbecue grills pose both a fire hazard and the risk of exposure to carbon monoxide.

Charcoal Grills:

- Purchase the proper starter fluid and store out of reach of children and away from heat sources.
- Never add charcoal starter fluid when coals or kindling have already been ignited.
- Never use any flammable or combustible liquid other than charcoal starter fluid to get the fire going.

Propane Grills:

- Check the propane cylinder hose for leaks before using it each time. A light soap and water solution applied to the hose will reveal escaping propane quickly by releasing bubbles.
- If you determined your grill has a gas leak by smell or the soapy bubble test and there is no flame:

    1. Turn off the propane tank and grill.

    2. If the leak stops, get the grill serviced by a professional before using it again.

    3. If the leak does not stop, call the fire department.

- If you smell gas while cooking, immediately turn off the grill, get away from it, and call the fire department. Do not attempt to move the grill.
- All propane cylinders manufactured after April 2002 must have overfill protection devices (OPD). OPDs shut off the flow of propane before capacity is reached, limiting the potential for release of propane gas if the cylinder heats up. OPDs are easily identified by their triangular-shaped hand wheel.
- Use only equipment bearing the mark of an independent testing laboratory. Follow the manufacturer instructions on how to set up the grill and maintain it.
- Never store propane cylinders in buildings or garages. If you store a gas grill inside during the winter, disconnect the cylinder and leave it outside.

Chapter 4

Food Spoilage—
Don't Make Yourself Sick

Check expiration dates on food items monthly. This includes cans, boxes, bottles, and spices—basically anything you consume. I cannot stress the importance of this enough. Food poisoning can kill you, so don't take this chapter lightly. When you reheat food, make sure you see steam rising from it so that any bacteria are killed during the heating process. There was a new study done in 2013 that found you can still use products after posted dates except Baby Formula, milk and fresh meats. Always conduct a "smell" test and an "eye" test. If the item smells odd or you can see mold, do not use.

Storage Times for Refrigerated Foods:
- Ground beef, turkey, veal pork, lamb, stew meats – 1 to 2 days
- Fresh meat – steaks, chops, roasts – 3 to 5 days
- Variety meats – tongue, kidneys, liver, heart, chitterlings – 1 to 2 days
- Fresh poultry (chicken or turkey – whole, part, giblets) – 1 to 2 days
- Bacon – 7 days
- Sausage, raw from meat or poultry – 1 to 2 days
- Smoked breakfast links, patties – 7 days
- Summer sausage labeled "Keep Refrigerated" – Unopened, 3 months; Opened, 3 weeks
- Hard sausage (such as Pepperoni) – 2 to 3 weeks

- Ham, canned, labeled "Keep Refrigerated" – Unopened, 6 to 9 months; Opened, 3 to 5 days
- Ham, fully cooked, whole – 7 days
- Ham, fully cooked, half – 3 to 5 days
- Ham, fully cooked, slices – 3 to 4 days
- Corned beef in pouch with pickling juices – 5 to 7 days
- Hot dogs – Unopened package, 2 weeks; Opened package, 1 week
- Luncheon meats – Unopened package, 2 weeks; Opened package, 3 to 5 days
- Store-prepared (or homemade) egg, chicken, tuna, ham, and macaroni salads – 3 to 5 days
- Pre-stuffed pork, lamb chops, and chicken breasts – 3 to 4 days
- Commercial brand vacuum-packed dinners with/USDA seal, unopened – 2 weeks
- Cooked meat, poultry and fish leftovers:
  o Pieces and cooked casseroles – 3 to 4 days
  o Gravy and broth, patties, and nuggets – 3 to 4 days
  o Soups and Stews – 3 to 4 days
- Fresh fish and shellfish – 1 to 2 days
- Eggs: (Do not put them in the front or in the door or they will spoil earlier. Keep eggs in the back of the fridge, where it is the coldest.)
  o Fresh, in shell – 3 to 5 weeks
  o Raw yolks, whites – 2 to 4 days
  o Hard-cooked – 1 week
  o Liquid pasteurized eggs, egg substitutes – Unopened, 10 days; Opened, 3 days
  o Cooked egg dishes – 3 to 4 days

In the Fridge Once Opened:
- Baby food: last 1 to 3 days
- Pasta sauce: lasts 5 days
- Mayonnaise: lasts 2 months (1 ½ years after purchase if unopened)
- Cheese: lasts 1 to 4 weeks

- Leftovers: last 3 to 4 days
- Milk: throw it out once it reaches its expiration date or starts to sour (whichever comes first)

Pantry Items:
- Crackers/cereals: 9 months to 1 year if unopened
- Peanut butter: 3–4 years after buying if unopened
- Condiments: 1 ½ years after buying if unopened

Canned Food:
- High-acid foods such as tomatoes, fruit, and fruit juice can be stored for up to 18 months.
- Low-acid foods such as vegetables and meat can be stored for two to five years.

Frozen Food:
- Fruits and vegetables: 8 to 12 months
- Poultry: 6 to 9 months
- Fish: 3 to 6 months
- Ground meats: 3 to 4 months
- Cured or processed meat: 1 to 2 months
- Ice cream: 12 days to 2 months, depending on condition of freezer

Thawing Food:
- Refrigerator thawing - Take frozen food from the freezer and place in refrigerator over-night. (If you place the food in the refrigerator the night before you intend to cook, chances are that it will be thawed the next evening). Anything over 5 pounds you need to take 24 hours per 5 pounds to thaw. A major advantage of refrigerator thawing is that you don't have to cook the defrosted food right away. This is especially helpful if you're faced with a last-minute change in plans. Poultry, fish and ground meat that's been defrosted in the fridge can be kept for an additional 1 to 2 days in the refrigerator before cooking. Beef, pork, lamb or veal (roasts, steaks or chops) will keep refrigerated for

another 3 to 5 days after thawing. Another plus: If you decide not to cook the thawed food, you can safely refreeze it within these same time limits.

- Cold water thawing – The food must be placed in a leak-proof package or plastic bag. Submerge the bag in cold tap water. If the bag leaks, bacteria from the air or surrounding environment could be introduced into the food. Also, the meat tissue may absorb water, resulting in a watery product. Never use hot water, as that can cause the outer layer of the food to heat up to a temperature where harmful bacteria begins to multiply. You'll need to change the water every 30 minutes to ensure that it stays sufficiently cold. Food requires thirty minutes per pound for thawing. Once the food is thawed completely, you'll need to cook it immediately. If you have a change in plans, you can safely refreeze the food once you've cooked it thoroughly.
- Microwave thawing - When thawing food in a microwave, plan to cook it immediately after thawing. With microwave thawing, some areas of the food may become warm and begin to cook during the thawing process. This may bring the food to "Danger Zone" temperatures. Foods thawed in the microwave should be cooked before refreezing.
- It may be tempting to just leave your frozen food out on the cupboard to thaw — it's easy and it's fast. Don't do it. Also, never thaw foods in a garage, basement, car, dishwasher or plastic garbage bag; outdoors or on the porch. These methods can leave your foods unsafe to eat. Nor should you thaw food in hot water. The problem with both of those methods is that the outer layer of the food can sit between the bacteria breeding temperatures of 40°F and 140 °F for far too long to be safe.
- Cooking Without Thawing - When there is not enough time to thaw frozen foods, or you're simply in a hurry, just remember: it is safe to cook foods from the frozen state. The cooking will take approximately 50% longer than the recommended time for fully thawed or fresh meat and poultry.

Chapter 5

Simple Ways to Cut Costs

For many, the recent economic downturn has affected the way we purchase food and necessities, and in other areas of our life. Even singles that cook dinner at home most nights are struggling to afford the ingredients to make a healthy meal. We all want to maximize the value of our spending, but it isn't always easy.

Use What You Have First

Are you throwing your money in the trash each week? Do you have expired items in your pantry, freezer or refrigerator? Each time you toss those expired items in the trash you are throwing your money in the trash along with it. When you are grocery shopping are you buying too much? Perhaps the larger size may be more economical, but is it really worth the savings when you are throwing away portions of it because you cannot use it all and it has expired? If you shop with coupons, you can afford to buy the smaller size and cut the waste.

Before you go to the grocery store, check to see what you already have that you could use for the week. How many breakfast options do you have in your refrigerator, pantry or freezer? Can you get by another week without buying breakfast foods? Apply the same principle with lunch and dinner. Plan your meals for the week prior to going to the store, so that you know exactly what you already have and what you need. Don't go to the grocery store without a list. Those that shop with a list are more apt to spend less than those that go without one. When you have a list to concentrate on you are more focused. Make sure to clip your coupons and match them to your list. Do not buy items just because you have a coupon unless you know you will use them.

While at the grocery store, shop the perimeter of the store. The perimeters (outer sides) have the fresh items such as fruits, vegetables, milk, eggs, meats, etc. The outer perimeter is the healthiest part of the grocery store. You want to eat fresh to keep you and your family healthy. Also, by buying fresh fruits and vegetables you control how much you purchase, thereby limiting the amount of waste for the week. Take a good look around your grocery store and make note of what is in the middle isles versus the outer perimeter. You will notice that the middle isles contain the more "fattening" or "junk" foods. These are the items that you want to limit.

Spraying Dollars and Cents

Have you ever considered the amount of money you are throwing away with spray items such as sunscreen sprays? You are spraying the contents while the wind is blowing, thereby spraying yourself, others, water, and the sand. Instead of using deodorant sprays or hair spray, utilize alternatives. I'm not saying not to purchase these items. I just want you to be aware of the other options out there for you that will save you money in the long run. It has been determined that aerosol sprays are hurting our ozone layer, so let's protect our Earth. Go green when you can.

Other Cost Cutting ideas:
- Freeze cheese that starts going bad. Don't buy shredded cheese when you can shred it yourself.
- Whole or cut-up bone-in chicken can save money. Buy family size packs on sale and freeze individually. You can also bake extra and use for several days.

- Soak and cook dried beans to save money.
- Before vegetables go bad, freeze them or make soup.
- Cut and freeze fresh fruit when on sale or overripe. Use later in smoothies, oatmeal or yogurt. Freeze pureed fruit in ice cube trays. Once frozen, transfer to a freezer bag.
- Substitute yogurt for cream cheese or sour cream in recipes. To economize and reduce package waste, buy in volume and use small servings.
- Buy bread in bulk when on sale and freeze for later.
- Grow your own romaine lettuce by putting the "stub" (the bottom inch or two) in a glass of water near a sunny window. You can do the same thing with celery, spring onions, cabbage, bok choy and similar vegetables. For best results, cut a thin layer off the stub first.

High Nutritional Value at a Low Cost

- Raw cabbage is fewer than 10 cents a serving and has fewer calories than potatoes and is a great addition to salads, soups and stir-fries.
- Carrots, bananas, pears, watermelon and frozen broccoli, each at less than 30 cents a serving are all high in nutrition.
- Turkey and whole chicken offer high protein at low costs.
- Fresh, whole carrots and sweet potatoes are among the best produce buys, but frozen corn and broccoli almost always cost less than their fresh equivalents and are just as nutritious.
- A serving of oatmeal is half the cost of sugary processed cereals, plus it's more filling and causes less fluctuation in blood sugar levels. Avoid pricey oatmeal packets; they're often loaded with salt and sugar.
- Canned salmon is almost always wild caught and is more economical than fresh.
- *Queso Blanco*, a mild, soft, white cheese common in Latino cooking, is both less expensive and less processed than many other cheeses.
- Make eggs, brown rice and sweet potatoes an important part of your weekly diet.

Eating healthy doesn't have to be expensive. Watch for sales and remember to shop the perimeter of the store for healthier choices.

Save Money on Heating/Cooling:

- Trees and shrubs are a great way to shield your home from the elements. Trees reduce bills not just by shading your home, but by cooling the air by releasing moisture. Do not allow the trees or shrubs to touch the home to avoid unwanted pests.
- Check the seal on doors and windows. Feel around your doors and windows to see if air is coming in. It's hard to save money on heating/cooling if all of your money is going out the door or window. You can also get a professional to come in and assess this for you at minimal or no cost.
- Turn on your ceiling fan. Running your ceiling fan in the summer cools you, but running it in the opposite direction can help warm the room up by pushing warm air down into the room. Run the ceiling fan only when in the room. Did you know you can save up to $7.00 per month by turning off ceiling fans when you are out of the home?
- Heat only the rooms you need. Close off one room or section of the house to the rest to save money on heating. Concentrate your heat in the area that you will be spending the most time. You can put blankets up over doorways or at the foot of doors to help stop the heat from escaping.
- Run heat-generating appliances like ovens and dryers early in the morning or late at night. Or better yet, use a clothesline. A clothesline will save $100 a year versus running your dryer.
- Eat at home. While you cook the kitchen gets nice and warm, so cook and eat in there. It really doesn't add any unnecessary charge to your energy bill.
- Purchase a space heater. You can turn your thermostat down further and still sleep in a warm room thanks to a space heater that uses less energy. If you use a space heater, be sure to always read the manufacturer's directions and keep it a safe distance from other items in the room.

- Put extra covers on the bed for warmth or remove them to be cool. If you put extra covers on the bed, you won't need the thermostat as high (or low) at night.

Whether you are cutting costs because you want to or need to, the process should be manageable and positive. Consider turning these immediate changes into long-term habits to keep your overall spending low. Don't be too frugal and say no to everything because you are more likely to give up if that happens. Frugal living isn't about waiting for items you want to purchase. It is about spending less on the things that don't matter to you as much, so you can spend more money and time on the things that do matter.

Chapter 6

Preventing Pests and Bugs

No person wants to see unwanted pests in the home. This includes roaches, spiders, ants, flees, and mice. If you have pets in the home, be careful what you leave on the floor. Do not leave poisons out in the open. Make sure to limit where your pets eat and drink and pick up bones and chewy toys when not in use. Do not let your pet hide dog biscuits in the couch, chairs, blankets, or bed, as this could attract unwanted pests. Make sure to wash pet items often.

Limit Where You Eat:
- Eat only in kitchen and dining room areas.

Clean the Floor Daily:
- Pick up what you spill and wipe the area clean with a damp cloth.

Wash Dishes:
- Do not let dirty dishes stay in the sink for a long period of time.
- Clear the drain area after rinsing dishes.

In the Pantry:
- Wipe down bottles and jars after use.
- Store food properly—it is best to keep sugar and flour in the refrigerator.

- Keep rice, pasta, and cereals in plastic containers that seal tightly.

Throw Out Old Foods and Vegetables:
- Throw out foods and vegetables when they are past their prime, especially bananas and tomatoes. Remember to freeze them before you have to toss them.

In the Closet:
- Clean clothes before storing them.
- Mothballs use an insecticide to kill pests, so make sure to place them high on a shelf out of the reach of children.

In the Garbage:
- Rinse out recyclables.
- Rinse out garbage containers (both outside and inside containers).
- Keep a lid on the trash.

Outside Areas:
- Do not store wood inside.
- Trim back foliage near the house (do not allow branches/bushes to touch the house).
- Avoid standing water (especially in toys).
- Check your screens and repair broken ones so the bugs cannot get in.
- Make sure the doors and windows are sealed properly.
- In place of expensive bug zappers, hang a fabric softener sheet adjacent to, but not touching, outdoor light fixtures to keep flying insects like mosquitoes and moths away. They hate the scents generated when the softener sheets are heated.
- Keep deer away. Pouring a rotten egg cocktail around your plants will keep deer from eating them. Just mix six raw eggs in two gallons of water and let it sit outside for a week then just pour around plants.

Exterminating Pests:

- If you have unwanted pests, get rid of them immediately.
- Make sure to use the appropriate bug spray as indicated on the can and/or spray bottle.
- For mice, use a mouse trap with peanut butter on it.
- Check your local supermarket for other types of pest removal items.
- If you use a poison, make sure it is out of reach of children and pets.
- Keep a "fly-swatter" handy in the kitchen area but away from food.
- If you do swat a fly, clean up the area with an antibacterial wipe.
- Kill fleas and flea eggs embedded in pillows, blankets or throw rugs by placing these items in a plastic garbage bag and placing the bag in your car with the windows rolled up for a couple of hours when it's hot outside. The extreme heat will kill the fleas.

Chapter 7

Clean Clothes and Stubborn Stains

Laundry is no one's favorite thing to do, but if you are going to do it, do it from start to finish. When you have company over, you really do not want to have clean clothes piled up on a chair or couch (or floor) waiting to be folded and put away. Also, if you remove the clothes from the dryer right away, you could cut down on ironing or steaming. Don't waste electricity by tossing clothes back in the dryer to get the wrinkles out.

If your clothes are not drying as fast you think they should, check the dryer vent to see if it is clogged with lint. Be sure to check the vent outside of the home to make sure it is not covered over by something and you can feel the air coming out. If that is not the problem, then have a repairman check to see if the dryer heating element needs to be replaced.

Check tags on clothing to see how they should be washed. There is nothing worse than washing something that should have been dry cleaned. It shrinks and you can no longer wear it. If it says to hand wash, then wash it in the sink or tub. Make sure to check the temperature that it should be hand washed in. Invest in a small clothesline (from your local hardware or department store) that you can string in the bathroom, or hang clothes on the shower rod to dry.

Laundry:

- Keep up with laundry. Do not allow yourself to fall behind.
- Try to do laundry when you have at least one color load and one white load.
- Wash colors in cold water and use the easy care or permanent press dryer setting.
- Wash whites in warm water and use the cotton dryer setting.
- Keep laundry items (laundry soap, dryer sheets, and stain remover) on a shelf, not on the washer or dryer.
- Empty lint tray after each dryer use.
- Wipe top of washer and dryer once a week with damp cloth.
- Pour a cup of white vinegar into the bottom of an empty washer once a month and run a normal cycle. It keeps your washer clean and smelling fresh.

Stain Removal:

- Treat the area immediately.
- Remove as much of the stain as you can by blotting the fabric with tap water or soda water.
- Pre-treat with a pre-wash stain remover.
- For dry powder stains, reach for a soft brush before the wet cloth. Never add water to stains that are formed solely from dry powder.
- Use only white cloths to blot up spills. A color cloth or napkin could create another stain.
- Use cold water to wash stains under the tap.
- If you are out to dinner and encounter a stain, blot it with soda water and a white cloth napkin.
- Take the item to a drycleaner, who is likely to have encountered the problem before.
- Mask the damage. Try wearing stained shirts only under jumpers, or turn up hems/cuffs where feasible.
- For carpets stains, you could cover with additional area rugs.
- For cushions and tablecloth stains, try adding trimmings, bows or badges. As an alternate, dye the fabric or paint over hard surfaces.

- Before using a carpet stain remover, test a small portion of carpet in an area where no one can see it.

Ironing/Steaming:

- Read the manufacturer's instructions before using an iron or steamer, especially for the product care instructions.
- Make sure you understand the hazards associated with use of the iron and/or steamer.
- Do your ironing in the bedroom. You will be able to use the bed to sort your laundry, and you will have hangers close at hand in the closet.
- Pay attention at all times to what you are doing. Do not leave the iron on or unattended. Most new irons today have an auto shut off, but it is best not to take chances.
- Fill the water compartment of your iron to the full line with cool water. Some irons recommend distilled water, which is a good idea if your tap water is hard.
- Make sure your ironing board has a cover pad. If you do not have an ironing board, then you can lay a towel (folded once) over a tile floor or carpet and iron on that. Do not use a laminate counter top or a wood floor. If using a cover, place your ironing board cover on the board while it is still damp, and let it dry in place.
- You can cut your ironing time by putting a piece of aluminum foil under the ironing board cover. The foil will reflect heat so you are actually ironing from both sides at once.
- Start with articles of clothing that need the lowest temperature and move on to those requiring the highest temperature.
- Check the wash care tag on the garment for the type of fabric it is. Use only the settings for that type of fabric.
- Test a small area to make sure that the iron is not too hot for the garment.
- To prevent collars, cuffs, and hems from puckering, iron them on the wrong side first.
- Long-sleeve shirts: If you do not have a sleeve board, insert a rolled-up towel in the sleeves so they can be pressed without leaving creases.

- To avoid flattening embroidery or eyelets when ironing, iron them face down on a thick towel.
- Hold pleats in place with paper clips when ironing. Be careful that the clips do not snag the fabric, particularly if it has a loose weave.
- Use the tip of the iron to work around buttons and the corners on the sleeves.
- Hang your shirts up promptly on a hanger after ironing to keep them from wrinkling. Be sure to button the top and center buttons.
- Make sure your iron is hot enough for your fabric but not too hot. A too-cool iron will not remove all the wrinkles, and one that is too hot can scorch or otherwise damage your fabric.
- Delicate fabrics may need to be ironed using a press cloth. A clean white towel will work.
- When you are finished ironing, make sure to empty the water from your iron while the iron is hot. This will reduce the moisture in the water compartment.
- Allow the iron to cool before you put it away. It is best to set the iron on the stove to allow it to fully cool.
- Never leave the iron plugged in. This could cause a tripping hazard and can also be hazardous to small children, as they might turn it back on and burn them.
- Always keep your ironing board cover clean and in good condition. Damage to the cover may transfer to your garments.
- If you are not big on ironing, invest in a small garment steamer. They work just as well. Be careful with the steam because it gets really hot and can burn you.
- Make sure to check the label to see if the garment can be steamed.
- For steaming, do small strokes from top to bottom on the fabric. When finished with the steamer, unplug and store as usual.

Chapter 8

Simply Sewing

I learned to sew when I was in the Girl Scouts. It was a good thing because my home economics class did not cover as much as I would have liked. When I was a young mother, I used to make my kids' clothes. When things are homemade, they are extra special because the person who made them cared enough to do so. There are department stores that sell items for less than you can make them, but that does not mean they are made well. You have to at least know how to fix a hem, sew on a button, or mend a hole. If you are not comfortable in learning this, the good news is that many dry cleaners and/or seamstresses offer these services for you. There are physical examples of how to create these stitches demonstrated on the Internet, which is especially helpful if you learn by seeing something done.

Sewing Supplies:
- Different colors of threads
- Needles
- Scissors
- Sewing basket for storage

Sewing Basics:
- Everyone needs to know how to fix a seam and sew on a button. There's no need get rid of clothes that can be fixed.

- Do not be intimidated by sewing—it really isn't that hard.
- Pick a color of thread closest to the fabric.
- Keep needles out of reach of children.
- Insert thread into needle eye (small hole at the end) and tie a knot on one end of the thread so that it stops in the fabric when inserted.

Hand Stitches:

- Running stitch is the simplest of stitches, where the thread runs straight through the fabric without doubling back on itself. It is used to join fabric for gathering and mending.
- Basting stitch is similar to the running stitch but has very long stitches. It's used as a flexible alternative for pinning and for gathering. It can be pulled out easily.
- Back stitch is a strong stitch that is formed by pulling the needle through the fabric and then doubling it back on itself. The needle emerges beyond the stitch just made and doubles back again for the next stitch. Works well for hems.
- Whip stitch is a basic over and over stitch that can be used to form a hem or seam.
- To sew on a button: place the button on the material where you intend to sew it in place. Push the needle through the material and up through one of the holes in the button. Push the needle down through a different hole in the button. Repeat these steps going up through the material and button holes so that each hole is secured by multiple strands of thread. It is best to do this in an X fashion. Tie off thread closest to material and cut the thread.
- You can tie off your sewing thread by creating a loop. Pull your thread through the loop; grasp the thread just behind the needle after it is through the loop, and pull to tighten the loop. This leaves a second loop with which to thread through again. Pull your thread through that second loop and tighten the knot. Cut the thread.

Chapter 9

Keeping You Well

It would be nice to have a full-time doctor or nurse in the home, but most of us are not that lucky. I have included some basic information on common items/illnesses that you may encounter. Just remember that when something happens, do not panic. There is a solution to most every problem.

Take a CPR (Cardio-Pulmonary Resuscitation) and Basic First Aid Course, especially if you intend to have children or help others to care for children. Below are some guidelines that I follow. I am a medical professional (Registered Nurse) but not a physician, so please make sure to check with your physician before implementing these suggestions. What works for one person does not always work for another.

Health Insurance:
- By now, we all know health insurance is not optional. You need to carry some type of health insurance on yourself and your family.
- Compare rates with different companies before deciding.
- Make sure you fully understand the coverage and the deductible.
- If you cannot afford to purchase medical coverage check into one of the many affordable or possibly free programs from the state and/or federal government.

Medications:

- Try to limit the amount of medications that you use. Certain medications cannot be taken with other medications. Make sure that your doctor and pharmacist know exactly what you are taking, even the over-the-counter medications.
- Mixing medications can be fatal.
- Do not take another person's medication. If it was prescribed for them, it may be a different dosage than what you need and may not mix well with what you are already taking.
- If your medication says you can take it on an empty stomach, eat something with it just in case. Everyone reacts differently, so be cautious.
- Tight on a budget? Ask your doctor about prescription samples.
- Transfer prescriptions to a new grocery or drugstore when it offers a gift card for store credit, and use that to pay for your purchases.

Wellness:

- General Practitioner: yearly visit for checkup or physical
- Gynecologist: once a year
- Dentist; every six months for cleaning (otherwise at least once a year)
- Eye exam: every two years
- Dermatologist: once a year to check for skin cancer (moles)
- Breast/Testicular exams: once a month
- Mammograms: as directed by your physician (according to age and history)
- Colonoscopy: as directed by your physician (according to age and history)
- Try yoga. It's good for both your body and your mind. Look for free classes in your area.
- Replace all tooth brushes (or tooth brush heads for those electronic) every three months or immediately after an illness once you complete your antibiotics.

Sickness:

- Call your doctor if you have a fever of 101°F or higher.

- Nausea/vomiting: do not eat or drink anything for at least four hours.
- Once you start eating and/or drinking, start slowly with small sips and crackers.
- If you do not feel better within twenty-four hours, call your doctor.
- Bee stings: if you feel your throat swelling up and you have difficulty breathing, call 911 or get someone to take you to the nearest emergency room. If you only have a local reaction (burning, itching, redness and tenderness), you can mix a paste of tobacco, baking soda, and water and place it on the site for fifteen to twenty minutes. When removing a stinger, never use tweezers, fingers, or anything that will compress the end of the stinger, as a venom sack is still attached to it. This will cause the venom left in the sack to be injected into the wound. The proper way to remove a stinger is to take a credit card or other flat, ridged, thin object and scrape the stinger off the skin.
- Headache: put a cold compress to the back of the neck for twenty minutes at a time.
- Strong headache or migraine: drink a tall glass of water. Many headaches are due to dehydration. If the pain does not subside after twenty minutes, take a pain reliever.
- Take a pain reliever for fever, aches, and/or pain.
- Take an over-the-counter medication for cold and allergy symptoms.
- Take an antacid for an upset stomach or heartburn/indigestion.
- Know the difference between heartburn and a heart attack. If you think you are having a heart attack, seek medical attention immediately.
    - **Chest discomfort.** Most heart attacks involve discomfort in the center of the chest that lasts more than a few minutes, or that goes away and comes back. It can feel like tight pressure, squeezing, fullness or pain. In women, the discomfort can occur in any area of the chest.
    - **Discomfort in other areas of the upper body.** Symptoms can include pain or discomfort in one or both arms, the back, neck, jaw or stomach.

     o **Stomach pain**. Sometimes people mistake stomach pain that signals a heart attack with heartburn, the flu, or a stomach ulcer. Other times, women experience severe abdominal pressure that feels like an elephant sitting on your stomach.

     o **Shortness of breath**. May occur with or without chest discomfort.

     o **Other signs:** These may include breaking out in a cold sweat, nausea or lightheadedness.

- Increase your fluid intake and take Vitamin C when you feel a cold coming on.
- Check medication expiration dates on prescription and over the-counter medications every six months and before you take it.
- Never leave any type of medication in a hot car. It will alter the effectiveness.
- When in doubt, go get checked out!

Smoking:

- If you have small children in the home, second hand smoke has the same nicotine and other toxic chemicals that you are taking in.
- Children exposed to secondhand smoke are at an increased risk of sudden infant death syndrome (SIDS), acute respiratory infections, ear problems, and more severe asthma. Smoking by parents causes breathing (respiratory) symptoms and slows lung growth in their children.
- If you smoke, please quit. Quit not only for yourself, but for your loved ones.

Chapter 10

Eat Healthy—Be Healthy

Mealtime can be so frustrating. I remember when I was a newly-wed and wanted to make a nice dinner. I was nineteen years old and just did not have a lot of experience. I got a really nice cookbook as a wedding gift, so I decided to make the first meal I could find that looked easy. I remember it was a chicken dish. I also remember that it was the worst meal I ever had! So after that I stuck with what I could remember my mother making for dinner and kept it very simple.

Over the years I have learned to cook, but it was mostly due to trial and error. I have many store-bought cookbooks with lots of good recipes. However, over the years, I have made my own cookbook by cutting recipes out of magazines and placing them in a plastic cover sheet and putting them into a large binder. I use them more than anything and have made some really good meals.

I have found that by going to other peoples' homes that their idea of a meal and mine are pretty different. I was raised that you have a meat, starch, and a vegetable. However, I know a lot of that has changed. This could be a really large chapter, but for now I am going to provide you with some basics that I have learned along the way. Picture a triangle—this is your food pyramid. Hopefully this is just a review for you. The smallest area is at the top and the largest at the bottom. So when I say that something is on top or first, then you consume less of it, and when something is on the bottom or last, then you have more.

Nutrition Basics:
- Cooking can be fun. Relax. Enjoy.
- If you make a bad meal, do not give up. There is always takeout!
- Make sure to always have something "green" with your meal, like a vegetable or salad.
- Alcohol is not an appetizer.
- Take a multivitamin daily.
- Never skip breakfast. It really is the most important meal of the day.
- Diet pills do not count as a meal.
- Diet and exercise is the safest way to lose weight.
- Eat several small meals during the day rather than bingeing on large meals only three times per day.

Fats (these are at the top of the food pyramid, so use them sparingly):
- Fatty red meats
- Butter
- Refined grains such as white bread, white rice, pasta, and potatoes
- Sugary drinks and sweets
- Salt

Dairy (these are second on the food pyramid):
- Have 2 to 3 servings per day or take a vitamin D/calcium supplement
- Low fat/fat -free milk
- Low fat cheese
- Low fat/fat -free yogurt

Nuts, Seeds, Beans, Tofu (these are third on the food pyramid):
- Have 2 servings per day

- Almonds
- Walnuts
- Pecans
- Hazelnuts
- Pistachios
- Legumes (beans, lentils, soy, peanuts)
- Tofu

Fish, Poultry, Eggs (these share the third row of the food pyramid):
- Have 2 servings per day (5½ ounces of meat)
- Salmon, trout, and herring are rich in omega-3s, so keep them top on your list to eat.
- Chicken, without the skin
- Turkey, without the skin
- Eggs: best to eat only the egg whites

Vegetables and Fruits (these are the fourth row of the pyramid):
- Have 3 servings per day of vegetables
- Have 2 servings per day of fruits
- Lowers blood pressure
- Reduces your risk of having cardiac disease
- Reduces your risk of having cancer

Healthy Fats (these share the fourth row of the pyramid and consist basically of what you cook with or add to a dish):
- Unsaturated fats are healthy fats
- Avocados, nuts, seeds and fatty fish like salmon
- Oils: olive, canola, soy, corn, sunflower, peanut, and vegetable oil
- Trans-free margarine

Whole Grains (these also share the fourth row of the pyramid):
- Have 6 to 11 servings per day, depending on how active you are.
- Whole wheat pasta

- Oatmeal
- Whole wheat bread
- Brown rice
- Whole grain cereal
- Eating whole grains will help you feel less hungry, which will have a positive effect on your weight.

Daily Exercise and Weight Control (the last row and largest row of the pyramid):

- Drink at least 8 glasses of water per day.
- You do not have to be a member of a gym to exercise. A brisk walk for thirty minutes every day will help with weight control.

Serving Size Examples:

- Tip of your thumb = about one teaspoon of peanut butter
- Computer mouse = one serving of a baked potato
- CD (compact disc) = the serving size of a waffle or pancake
- Checkbook = a 3-ounce serving of fish
- Rounded handful = ½ cup cooked or raw rice or pasta
- Baseball or size of your fist = one serving of vegetable or fruit
- Tennis ball = ½ cup of food or ½ cup ice cream
- Golf ball or large egg = ¼ cup of dried fruit or nuts
- Six dice or one domino = one serving of cheese
- Deck of cards or the palm of your hand = a serving of meat, fish, or poultry

Chapter 11

New Baby Basics

The first thing you should know is this: do not panic, you cannot break them! New babies don't come with instructions, but there is plenty of help out there, even if you just use the Internet. Just don't believe everything you read. Join a mother/baby group. It is always nice to associate with other moms who are going through the same thing as you. Hold your baby often. You cannot spoil a baby simply by holding them. Babies need cuddling and love to grow. Talk and read to your baby often. Cribs are made for a reason, so use them. Do not put your baby in bed with you, as you could roll over and cause suffocation. Always remember, your baby did not ask to be born. Your bundle of joy came into this world as a result of your actions, so take care of your baby the best you can. If you are stressed, ask a friend or relative to watch your baby for an hour or so to allow yourself to decompress. Do not take your stress out on your baby. It does not mean you are a bad parent if you take a break from your child. Below I have covered those issues that are most prominent in the first year. If you haven't done so yet, take a CPR (Cardio-Pulmonary Resuscitation) and Basic First Aid course.

Baby Checklist for the First Year:
Below is a baby checklist for the first year. Do not be overwhelmed with the list below and the associated cost of obtaining these items. Ask family, friends, and neighbors for their used items. Make sure the used items meet safety codes. (e.g., child car seats)

- Find a Pediatrician by getting referrals from friends. If you find a good one, keep him/her. If not, keep looking. You have to be comfortable and so does your baby.
- A car seat is mandatory. Make sure to follow the National Guidelines on when to use car seats versus booster seats. Optional gear includes a stroller, highchair, and gym or play arches.
- Mandatory furniture includes a crib and crib mattress. Optional furniture or equipment includes a playpen/play yard, changing table, dresser, and rocker.
- Clothing: one-piece outfits, one-piece pajamas, socks, and booties, fleece outfits/sweaters or jacket for winter, mittens, bonnet or cap for summer, and shoes.
- Diapering: you'll need plenty of diapers (cloth or disposable), wipes, washcloths, diaper ointment/powder, and a sealable trash can.
- Feeding: Bibs, bottles, and nipples (if not breast feeding), plastic spill mats for around highchair, plastic bowls, plastic sippy cups, and rubber-tipped baby spoons.
- Bath: you'll need a baby tub, tub seat, slip-resistant bath tub mats, a tub spout cover, washcloths, soaps, lotions, and hooded towels.
- Sleep: you'll need a waterproof crib/mattress liner, fitted sheets and receiving blankets.
- Safety: For infants install smoke alarm/carbon monoxide detectors. Purchase a digital thermometer, first aid kit (which includes nasal aspirator, baby nail clippers, and Infant Pain Reliever), safety gates, outlet covers, toilet seat latches, and bumpers for sharp-cornered objects. Optional equipment is a baby monitor.
- For mom: you'll need nursing bras, breast pads, breast shields, cream for nipples, and panty liners/pads.
- Miscellaneous: small lamp or nightlight for baby's room, classical or lullaby music, reference books, books you can read to your baby, and baby laundry soap.

Immunizations:

Have these done according to the schedule that your Pediatrician establishes. The Pediatrician should follow the National Guidelines.

Fever:

If a newborn baby (newborn to 3 months) has a fever of 100.5 or higher, call the Pediatrician. You can use a digital thermometer or a glass mercury thermometer. It is best to have separate thermometers if you plan to use in different areas such as Rectal, Oral and Axillary. Below are the recommended steps on how to use a digital rectal thermometer.

- Look for a rectal thermometer that has a flexible tip and a wide handle that doesn't let you insert it more than an inch. (If you were to accidentally insert the thermometer too far — if your baby gets very squirmy, for example — you could perforate your baby's rectum.)
- To prepare the thermometer, clean the end with rubbing alcohol or a little soap and warm water. Rinse with cool water. Then coat the end with a little petroleum jelly for easier insertion or use a disposable sleeve made for that purpose.
- Hold your baby on your lap, tummy down and bottom up, letting his legs dangle over the side of your thigh. Or place him on his back, either on the bed or on a changing table. Your baby may be more comfortable in the tummy-up position, since he's used to lying that way for diaper changes. Besides, you'll be better able to distract him if he can see your face.
- Press the thermometer button to turn it on. With your other hand, spread your baby's buttocks apart. Gently insert the bulb about half an inch to an inch (1.3 to 2.5 centimeters) into his rectum, or until the tip of the thermometer disappears.
- Keep a firm grip on his buttocks by cupping them with the palm and fingers of the hand that's holding the thermometer. Don't let go of the thermometer, or it may not stay in place if your baby starts wriggling. Never leave the baby unattended with the thermometer inserted.
- When the thermometer beeps, remove it and read your baby's temperature. Be aware that inserting anything into your baby's rectum can stimulate his bowels, so don't be surprised if

he poops when you take the thermometer out. Clean the thermometer with soapy water or rubbing alcohol, then rinse and dry before storing.

- Regardless of which method you use, don't take your baby's temperature right after he's had a bath, as it could affect his temperature. Wait at least 20 minutes after bath time for an accurate reading.

Diaper Rash Treatments (be sure to call you Pediatrician if you cannot control the rash):

- Make frequent diaper changes, wiping baby's bottom with warm water cloth instead of "baby wipes."
- Use barrier or blocking ointments. Avoid talcum powder—ointments are better.
- Fresh air: let baby spend some time without the diaper on (make sure to place your baby on a waterproof pad).
- Try other types of diapers.
- Avoid generic diapers when possible.
- Avoid soaps and other irritants. Baby wipes can dry out a baby's bottom.

Diaper Rash Prevention:

- Fresh air.
- Cleanliness: change as soon as your baby soils the diaper.
- Introduce new foods carefully.
- Use mild detergents preferably those made for babies.

Teething Signs/Symptoms:

- Irritability
- Drooling
- Chin rash
- Biting and gnawing
- Cheek rubbing and/or ear pulling
- Diarrhea (loose bowel movements)
- Low-grade fever
- Not sleeping well
- Cold like symptoms (runny nose)

Easing Teething Pain:

- Try teething rings, and water-filled and chilled rubber teething toys.
- Your fingers can provide counter pressure that can sometimes bring relief. Rub your baby's gums with your finger (make sure you wash your hands first).
- Offering your baby a cold bottle of water can also help. If sucking on the bottle bothers your child, offer a cold cup of water. The water can also help replenish your baby's fluid if there is excessive drooling or many loose bowel movements.

Colic Signs/Symptoms (call your Pediatrician if your child suffers from one or more of the following):

- Loud and continuous crying that can last from one to three hours at a time and occur about three or four days a week.
- Although the crying can happen at any time, most colicky babies cry more in the late afternoon or evening.
- Baby's face gets red.
- Legs are pulled up to the stomach and then may be fully stretched out.
- Feet may be cold.
- Hands may be clenched.
- Some babies refuse to eat or become fussy soon after eating.
- Has difficulty falling and staying asleep.
- Baby may lift her head or legs and pass gas.
- Baby may seem generally uncomfortable and appear to be in pain.

Easing Colic Symptoms:

- Keep a diary of when your baby cries, along with activities like napping, feeding and playing. Look for patterns that may offer a small clue to the solutions.
- If you are breast-feeding, try to eliminate dairy from your diet along with other gas-producing foods such as onions, cabbage, cauliflower, spicy foods, caffeine, and beans. Before eliminating dairy from your diet, be sure to check with your doctor first. Your doctor may not want you to eliminate dairy from your diet or he may want you to take calcium supplements.

- If you are bottle-feeding, do your best to reduce the amount of air that your baby swallows. Try using a curved bottle or a bottle with collapsible disposable liners.
- If your baby seems to have a lot of gas, hold the baby upright and burp frequently.
- Do not over feed your baby. This may actually make the colic worse. Stick to your normal feeding routine.
- If you are bottle-feeding, talk with your Pediatrician about changing formulas to a hypo-allergenic formula or soy formula.
- Take your baby to a part of your home that will provide less stimulation. Bright lights, noise, or a large number of people may further aggravate the colic.
- Wrap your baby up snugly in a blanket while walking around in a smooth steady motion (not an aggressive, bouncing motion).
- Go for a walk in a stroller or for a drive in the car.
- Give your baby a warm bath or place a warm water bottle on your baby's stomach. Be sure the bottle is not hot.
- Try rocking your baby in a rocking chair, or swinging her in a baby swing.
- Give your baby a gentle tummy massage.
- Some babies' like rhythmic sounds such as a vacuum cleaner, dishwasher, or clothes dryer and will calm down when they hear these types of sounds.

Ear Infection Signs/Symptoms (please note: there may not be significant signs, so call your Pediatrician if you are suspicious of an ear infection):

- Your baby pulls, grabs, or tugs at his ears. This may be a sign he is in pain. However, babies do pull on their ears for all kinds of reasons or for no reason at all, like discovering that they have ears!
- Diarrhea: the bug that causes the ear infection can cause loose bowel movements.
- Reduced appetite: ear infections can cause tummy upset. They can also make it painful for your baby to swallow and chew. You may notice your baby pull away from the breast or bottle after he takes the first few sips.

• A yellow or whitish fluid draining from the ear. This does not happen to most babies, but it is a sure sign of infection. It also signals that a small hole has developed in the eardrum. Do not worry—normally this will heal by itself once the infection is treated.

Daycare Information:

• If you plan on returning to work after having your baby, make sure to check out several daycares available in your area before making a decision.
• Try to make "pop in" visits to see what is happening during the day.
• You may need to make an appointment to see the daycare because they may not allow you to just show up.
• Make sure to get a list of what is included in the price and what you need to bring.
• Write your child's name on every item.
• Request that none of your baby's items be shared.
• Get a written schedule for the day.
• Make sure you understand the drop off and pick up procedure.
• Give the daycare a list of who can and cannot pick up the child.
• If possible, find a daycare where the front doors are kept locked.
• Ask what type of education they require of their staff.
• Are the staff members CPR (Cardio-Pulmonary Resuscitation) certified?

Last, but not least, start a savings plan for college. Ask your Accountant or Investment Counselor (Financial Advisor) for the plans available in your state.

Chapter 12

Keeping the Kids Well

The health and wellness of your child should not be taken lightly. Routine checkups are important to keep track of their proper growth and development. Health insurance is not an option for your child. You must have a good health plan. If you cannot afford a plan, check with your local or state agencies (Agency for Health Care Administration or Health and Human Services Agency) to see what they offer. Also check with your child's school to see if they offer some type of health plan.

Make sure to have emergency phone numbers (Pediatrician, Poison Control, your cell phone number, etc) displayed in an area where it is visible to everyone, including a babysitter.

Try to limit the amount of medications your children take. You do not want their tolerance level to be compromised. Try not to give aspirin-containing products on an empty stomach. If it bothers your stomach, it could bother theirs. As I stated earlier, I am a Registered Nurse but not a physician, so please make sure to check with your Pediatrician before implementing my suggestions. What works for one person may not always work for another. Below I have covered topics that I found most common in childhood.

Wellness:
- Checkups as deemed by Pediatrician.
- Dentist: every six months for cleaning (or at least once a year).

- Eye exam: as directed by Pediatrician.
- Listen to your child. If he or she says it hurts, it hurts.
- Teach your child not to share combs, brushes, hats, or scarves to prevent from getting lice.
- Teach your child not to share drinks and eating utensils to prevent illness (especially mononucleosis).

Sickness:

- Fever over 104°F is considered a medical emergency. Go to your nearest hospital Emergency Room.
- If your child over 3 months has a fever of 101°F or higher, place the child in a warm water bath to bring fever down. Call the Pediatrician to see if they want to see the child based on other symptoms that may be present, such as irritability, lethargy (difficult to wake up), diarrhea or vomiting.
- Give children pain relief medication as directed.
- If the fever does not come down after the bath and pain reliever, call the Pediatrician.
- For bleeding: apply pressure for 20 minutes to stop bleeding. If it does not stop, go to the emergency room.
- Cuts and scrapes: for minor cuts, use antibiotic cream and bandage. For major cuts, apply pressure and go the emergency room.
- Bumps to head: if your child loses consciousness, call 911.
    - o If there is no loss of consciousness, check to make sure that the pupils (the black area of eye) are equal and the size changes according to light exposure. You can do this with a flashlight. Light should make them smaller and darkness should make them larger.
    - o If your child is vomiting, go to emergency room.
    - o If your child is very sleepy after the bump or goes to sleep, go to the emergency room.
    - o If you think your child is okay, continue to watch. Make sure to awaken the child every two hours during the night to ensure the child is alert.
- Chicken pox: control fever, apply anti-itch medication, and soak in oatmeal bath. The most important thing is to keep your child

comfortable. Do not expose other children to your child while the pox areas are still oozing or wet. Apply mittens if necessary to keep your child from scratching. The incubation period of chicken pox is between ten and twenty days.

- Ear pain or ear drainage: call the Pediatrician.
- Bleeding from the ear: go to the emergency room.
- Throat pain: if your child has really bad breath, stomach pain and/or fever call the Pediatrician. If you can see white dots in the back of the throat, call the Pediatrician for an appointment, as this may be a strep infection.
- If you think your child has a broken limb (arm/leg), do not move it. Try to mobilize by putting a splint to keep it from moving and get to the nearest emergency room (or call 911). If there is a break and a bone is exposed, call 911. Do not try to move the limb.
- Ringworm: highly contagious, so do not share clothes, towels, bed sheets, or sports gear.
    - o Get treatment for ringworm right away to keep other family members from getting it.
    - o If you think you have been exposed to ringworm, wash your clothes in hot water with an anti-fungal soap.
    - o Change socks and underwear at least once per day.
    - o Wear loose-fitting cotton clothing. Avoid tight underwear, pants, and panty hose.
    - o If the ringworm is on the feet (also known as "athletes foot"), dry your child's feet last after showering and make sure to be careful when putting on underwear so the feet do not touch the underwear and spread it to the groin. Also wear slippers or sandals in locker rooms, showers, and public bathing areas.
    - o Keep skin clean and dry.
    - o Try to prevent your child from scratching and spreading the fungi.
    - o Take your pet to a veterinarian if they have patches of missing hair, which may be a sign of a fungal infection. Household pets can spread fungi that cause ringworm.

- Check medication expiration dates on prescription and over-the-counter medications every six months and before you give the medication to your child.
- When all else fails and you are not sure what to do, call the Pediatrician or go to the nearest emergency room. Better to be safe than sorry.

Chapter 13

Healthy Eating Habits for Kids

The best way to encourage your children to eat healthy is to set a good example. Parents and other family members should eat only healthy food. You should limit the amount of junk food and other items that are not as nutritional. If it is not in the house, they will not have easy access to it. You cannot always control what they eat when they are out of the house, so make sure that you provide the most nutritious food for them at home. This is not an all-inclusive list of the foods available to eat; however, it does provide you with a lot of healthy suggestions.

Grain Group - Grains have carbohydrates, which give the energy needed to run, play, sleep, learn, and grow:

- 5 servings per day
- Whole wheat pasta
- Oatmeal
- Whole wheat bread
- Brown rice
- Whole grain cereal
- Pancakes

Milk Group - Calcium is very important for children—it will strengthen bones, helps stop bleeding, and helps muscles contract and relax:

- 3 servings per day
- Milk
- Yogurt (including frozen yogurt)
- Cheese (string, block)
- Pudding

Vegetable Group – Many vegetables have vitamins and fiber important for digestion and have healing properties:

- 4 servings per day
- Greens: broccoli, peas, green beans, lettuce, celery, peppers
- White: cauliflower, potatoes, mushrooms
- Yellow: corn, squash
- Orange: sweet potatoes, carrots, carrot juice
- Red: peppers and tomato juice

Fruit Group - Fruits contain vitamins and fiber important for eyesight, healthy skin, and digestion:

- 3 servings per day
- Apples, bananas, oranges, pears, grapes, kiwi, pineapple, papayas
- Berries: strawberries, raspberries, blueberries
- Melons: watermelon, cantaloupe, honeydew

Meat/Protein Group - Meat helps build strong muscles, carries oxygen to all parts of the body, and prevents infection and anemia:

- 2 servings per day
- Beef (lean cuts)
- Pork
- Chicken and turkey (without the skin)
- Fish
- Dried beans and peas
- Peanut butter
- Eggs
- Nuts

Others - These foods are okay to eat in moderation and should not replace any previously listed foods:

- Fats, oils, spreads
- Candy, cookies, cakes
- Chips and other salty snacks
- Condiments
- Soda, tea, coffee

Exercise:

- Children should get at least sixty minutes of physical activity every day.
- Limit television time by planning TV watching in advance so they are not surprised when you turn the TV off.
- Limit video game time by setting a time limit for how long they can play. Use a kitchen timer so they know you are being fair and honest.
- Exercise as a family. Try biking, walking, playing ball, shoot hoops, walk the dog, or go to the park.
- Do not just send them out to play—go play with them!

Chapter 14

Landing a Job

Are we so busy trying find the right job that we forget how dress for the interview? Are we making sure our resume is complete and accurate? I worked as an Employment Recruiter for two years. Most times the applicants were on time and presented themselves in a professional manner. However, there were some that were late, unprepared, and looked as if they were going to the beach shortly after the interview.

Crafting Your Resume

Recruiters spend an average of four to six minutes on a resume. For many it only takes six seconds to check for key words that would indicate if a potential candidate will be scheduled for an interview. A good resume includes (or excludes) the following:

- No crazy fonts, colors, pictures - anything that's going to distract them from the content.
- It's important to include all your contact information on your resume so employers can easily get in touch with you. Include your full name, street address, city, state, and zip, home phone number, cell phone number, and email address.
- Many employers want to check a potential employee's social media site(s). It is up to you if you want to include these up front.

- A resume headline (also known as a resume title) is a brief phrase that highlights your value as a candidate. Located at the top of your resume, a headline allows a hiring manager to see quickly and concisely what makes you the right person for the job.
- If you include an objective on your resume, it's important to tailor your resume objective to match the job you are applying for. The more specific you are, the better chance you have of being considered for the job you are interested in.
- The experience section of your resume includes your employment history. List the companies you worked for, dates of employment, the positions you held and a bulleted list of responsibilities and achievements. Include dates of unemployment here as well to ensure all dates are accounted for. It's important to prioritize the content of your resume. List the most important and relevant experience first, with key accomplishments listed at the top of each position.
- In the education section of your resume, list the schools you attended, the degrees you attained, and any special awards and honors you earned. Include professional development coursework and certifications. Also include special memberships in clubs such as The National Honor Society, Future Business Leaders of America, etc.
- The skills section of your resume includes your abilities that are related to the job you are applying for. Include skills that are relevant to the position / career field that you are interested in. List items such as computer, software, social media, leadership and/or financial skills.
- Many people put "References available upon request" at the end of their resume. There is no need to include references on your resume or even to mention that references are available. Rather, have a separate list of references to give to employers upon request.

Technology is changing rapidly. Many companies are moving to online applications and online video interviews. In either case, how you present yourself on online will make or break your chance for a job. Preparation ahead of time is essential.

In all cases, be sure to personalize and customize your resume, so it reflects your skills and abilities and connects them with the jobs you are applying for. Check and recheck your resume for spelling errors. The best way to stand out in a negative way is to have spelling and grammatical errors.

Dress for the Part

What you wear to your next job interview might be more important than you think. First impressions are everything. Whether you like it or not, your appearance is the first thing people notice about you and this can play a big part in the hiring decision. You may only get one shot so you need to make it count.

Before going to that interview, do your homework on the company. Call the company's receptionist or Human Resource department and ask them what is recommended as far as dress code. The workplace has changed and many companies are embracing a more casual approach to what is appropriate office attire. If everyone at the office is wearing shorts and a T-Shirt and you arrive in a three-piece dark suit, you'll be out of place. However, don't dress too casual for the interview. Even if the company has a laid back dress code in general, they may expect you to dress up for the initial interview. Half the battle of interviewing is proving how you will be a part of the team. When in doubt, bring a jacket and you can dress up or dress down as you need.

Your appearance can give the perception of taking the opportunity seriously or give the impression you have a more casual attitude toward work and authority. It may also show you possess a lack of understanding of business etiquette. Here are some tips on what not to wear – no matter what:
- Skirts too short or too tight;
- Shirts with too much cleavage;
- Tight pants;
- Scuffed or broken shoes;
- Sneakers;

- Excessive makeup, perfume or cologne;
- Wearing pants below your behind showing your underpants;
- Clothes with holes, stains, snags, missing buttons or wrinkles;
- Jewelry that is too large, distracting, or flashy;
- Jeans.

Also:

- Make sure your nails are clean, cut and polished properly.
- Make sure you are well-groomed. Hair should be clean and styled. Women should wear make-up in a conservative manner. Save the heavy make-up for your date nights.
- Tattoos can be distracting during an interview. Cover them as best as possible until you know what the social norm is for the company.

The most important thing you bring or wear to an interview is your self-confidence. What you wear and how you wear will show that before you even have a chance to open your mouth.

Interviewing

The interviewing process can be stressful. Your first instinct is to tell them everything they want to hear so you can land the job. Make sure your resume is updated and have several copies in case there is more than one manager sitting in on the interview.

When you walk into an interview, there are certain questions that you can expect. Below is an example and possible responses. Be prepared for the main question: "Tell me about you." Keep your answer to a sentence or two to set you apart from other competitors. This is called your unique selling position (USP). Prepare your answer ahead of time by developing your own personal branding statement that clearly tells who you are and your major strengths. You must believe in what you have to offer or it will come across as rehearsed.

Question: What is your greatest strength?
Response: Discuss the attributes that will qualify you for the job. Do you have great time management skills? Highlight them here

with examples. Did you exceed sales goals at another position? Make sure to give specific examples.

Question: What is your greatest weakness?
Response: I don't think that we have weaknesses. I believe we have areas of improvement. Mention skills here that aren't critical for the job, skills you have improved on, and how you turn negative into positive. If the job will not require speaking in public, and you have a need for improvement here, then talk about that area of improvement. Put the focus on how well you work with others one on one. Always focus on the positive in the interview.

Question: Why did you leave your current job?
Response: Be direct and focus your interview answer on the future, especially if your leaving wasn't under the best of conditions. Never speak badly about a past employer. If you do this, the interviewer may wonder if you will be bad-mouthing his company next time you are interviewing with another company. Be honest and open and keep it brief. Most people leave an employer for a better opportunity. If this is the case, let them know. If you were fired, talk about how you were not a good match with your expertise in that company but you could be with this new company.

Question: Why do you want this job? Why should we hire you?
Response: This is where your research on the company will benefit you. You can speak to how your qualifications can make a difference. Talk about how the research you did matches your own short and long term goals and be prepared to talk about those goals. Give concrete examples of why your skills and accomplishments make you the best candidate for the position. Make sure your resume has key qualifications and experiences highlighted.

Question: Describe a difficult work project or situation and how you overcame it.
Response: Keep your answers positive. Talk about how you react to situations and not the stress of the situations. Give actual examples of situations that actually happened to you. Then discuss

what you did to solve the problem. Now is also a good time to talk about your time management skills and any courses you may have taken on handling stress.

Practice your responses to these questions so you sound positive, and clear, about your positions and your goals for the future. The key is to lead with your strongest benefit to the employer. Learn to separate yourself from the competitors and you will have a higher chance of being positively remembered and hired.

Time Management

Being able to manage your time is an important personal asset. Learning good time management skills takes time. Benjamin Franklin, one of the Founding Fathers of the United States, had twelve time management habits. Modern psychologists recognize three key elements in Franklin's three-hundred-year-old procedure for changing habits:

1. He started out committed to the new behavior.
2. He worked on only one habit at a time.
3. He put in place visual reminders.

You can use these habits in any order, but whatever you do, work on one each week. Although perfectionism is unattainable, you will see big improvements in your life.

Habit 1: Strive to be authentic.

Habit 2: Favor trusting relationships.

Habit 3: Maintain a lifestyle that will give you maximum energy.

Habit 4: Listen to your biorhythms and organize your day accordingly.

Habit 5: Set very few priorities and stick to them.

Habit 6: Turn down things that are inconsistent with your priorities.

Habit 7: Set aside time for focused effort. Make an appointment with yourself.

Habit 8: Always look for ways of doing things better and faster.

Habit 9: Build solid processes.

Habit 10: Spot trouble ahead and solve problems immediately.

Habit 11: Break your goals into small units of work, and think only about one unit at a time.

Habit 12: Finish what's important and stop doing what's no longer worthwhile.

Other tips to better manage your time:

- Get a grip on email. Try checking your email just three times a day. Train those around you to eliminate unnecessary emails and avoid "reply all."
- Limit meetings. Hold meetings only when necessary and keep them as brief as possible. Start on time, and people who are habitually late will quickly learn to show up on time.
- Use technology. There are apps to help you do everything faster, from scanning receipts to sharing contact information to taking notes and more.
- Delegate. Trying to do everything yourself is a common time waster.

If you're constantly wishing there were more than 24 hours in a day, stop and ask yourself if you are correctly utilizing the time management tips above. Make sure to get enough rest and exercise. It sounds senseless, but taking time out to exercise and get adequate sleep will give you the energy to get through the day more effectively and productively.

Social Media No-No's

Chances are you use social networking sites, or at least know someone who does. The fundamental function of most social networking sites is allowing "friends" to share information. Friends are people who have agreed to communicate with each other and allow each other some level of access to personal information. Anyone with access to the internet can join. Using these sites can help you find a job and connect with people who can assist you with growing your career. Did you know that utilizing these sites can have both a positive and a negative effect on your career? Social media when used the wrong way can jeopardize a job offer or even cause the loss of your current job.

Social media etiquette is often less about using manners and more about using your basic common sense. Be careful what you post about others because they in turn will post things about you. Here are some Do's and Don'ts on posting:

- Do think before "speaking." Just because something pops into your head, it doesn't mean it should be shared with the world. Think before posting.
- Do personalize messages and introductions. When you first connect with someone new, go ahead and introduce yourself. Let them know how you came across them and who you have in common. You might just make a great first impression.
- Do give back. Social media is a two-way street. Give as much positivity as you get. Better yet, give even more. It's all about networking.
- Do set your personal privacy settings on what can be shared and who can see your profile.
- Don't post questionable photos of others without their permission.
- Don't post questionable photos of yourself or your children. Social media sites are great for sharing good times, but posting that photo of yourself impaired at a party or other function only degrades you in other's eyes.
- Don't use social media while on the job, unless it is job related. Posting company business (good or bad) may get you into trouble. Posting inappropriate information on social media sites can also get you in trouble, or even cost you your job, especially when you do it from work.

Future employers, landlords, bank loan officers, colleges and others may request access to your social media sites to determine if you are a risk or a responsible person before they interact with you. Do they really need to see incriminating photos of you or read about your wild adventures? Remember everything comes up in a Google search, so be careful what you post. Don't believe me? Google your name and check out the results.

Chapter 15

Money Management

I had to learn a lot of this information the hard way. I hope that this advice will help you avoid making the same mistakes that I did as a young adult. It is basic information, but very important for you to know. If you do not have a sense of finance, then you could make big mistakes that could take years for you to recover from financially. Credit is a good thing, but having too many credit cards are not. I once had a total of thirteen credit cards with a combined overwhelming balance of fifty thousand dollars. Hence, I'm a good resource for this chapter.

Always know what you have in your accounts. This includes checking, savings, money markets, retirement accounts, and any other type of account that you deposit money into. If you have a retirement account through an employer and leave that employer, you can transfer your 401K or 403B into a retirement account at a financial institution of your choosing as long as you do not keep any of the money. If you keep some of the money, you are subject to taxes and penalties on that money. This information is not intended to replace financial advice already given by a professional accountant or tax advisor. There are many different types of financial investment firms available to assist you with your financial planning for retirement. Most are free through your employer, so take advantage of it.

Basics:

- "Pay yourself first." When you get paid, put 10% of your paycheck in a Savings Account.
- Keep a good credit score.
- Borrow only what you can afford.
- Live within your means.
- Always know what you owe.
- If you make the debt, own up to it and pay it any way you can. Bankruptcy should be your last option, not your first. Bankruptcy will stay on your credit for up to 15 years.
- Pay your bills on time. Mail the check at least seven days before due date. If you pay your bills online, then pay at least three days before the due date.
- Save your spare change in a large container. You would be surprised how fast it will add up.
- Shop around for the best banking interest rates.
- Bills, mail, and receipts can pile up. Go paperless wherever feasible by signing up to get bills and receipts online.
- Invest in a receipt scanner to keep track of paper receipts and keep everything on the computer. Just make sure to keep a good back up of your files.

Banking:

- Balance your checkbook once a month when the statement arrives. If you do not know how to balance a checkbook, look at the back of your bank statement and follow the directions. Basically you will cross off each cleared transaction with those in your check register. After you have completed this, take the ending balance on the statement and add any deposits that have not cleared then subtract any checks that have not cleared. The ending balance from the above should then match the balance in your check register.
- Check your bank account by phone or online at least once a week to make sure no one has stolen your identity and is using your card. Be careful utilizing online banking. If your security is not strong, hackers can steal your information while you are online.

- Know what the fees are for items such as Returned Checks, Check Holds, Overdrafts and other monthly account fee structures.
- Many financial institutions offer a service to notify you of suspicious activity on your bank/credit card. If you can afford this in your budget, take advantage of it.
- If your bank card is lost or stolen, either go to the nearest branch or call them immediately.
- When you use an automated teller machine (ATM), make sure you are aware of the people around you.
- If someone comes up behind you and demands money, give it to him or her and then report it to the bank and the police. Do not be a hero.
- Do not share your personal ID number (PIN) with anyone.
- Do not store your personal ID number where anyone can see it.

Credit Cards:

- You should have only one credit card. If you use your card, pay it off monthly. This will help to establish credit. Be on time with your payment.
- If you have a large balance, pay more than the required monthly payment to avoid high interest charges.
- Check credit card statements for charges to make sure they are yours.
- If your card is lost or stolen, check your statement for the number to contact and report it immediately.

Credit Score and Building Credit

The only way to build a credit history is to use credit. The key to building good credit is to use credit wisely. Whenever you submit an application for a loan, insurance or credit card, new information is added to your credit report. If you have little or no credit history, you can build credit responsibly over time.

- Check your credit report. In the United States, credit reports are maintained by three major credit reporting agencies:

Experian, Equifax and TransUnion. If you've never applied for any form of credit, then you shouldn't have an open file with any of these agencies. If you have an open file, contact the agencies immediately. It's possible that someone has already used your name and stolen Social Security Number to apply for credit.

- Once a year get your free credit report. There are several web sites that offer this service, however use a reputable site. You should not have to pay to get your score. Check your credit report for accuracy and don't be afraid to dispute information that isn't correct.

- Open a bank account. Lenders like to know that you have a few years of experience handling your own money and making regular withdrawals and deposits. They also like knowing that you have a steady income.

- Get a co-signer. The primary loan holder and cosigner share equal obligation for the debt, and the loan will appear on both your credit report and hers. As a result, it will help you build a credit history. Because the account and how it is paid will appear on both of your credit reports, it is essential that you make all of the payments on time. Any late payments will hurt both you and her.

- Pay your bills on time. (No explanation needed.)

- Get a secured credit card. A secured credit card is tied to collateral held in a bank account. In other words, your credit limit equals your checking account balance or another amount required by the card company. Although payments for purchases made with this card won't be drawn from your bank account. If you have $500 in the bank, then your credit limit for the card is $500. If you try to charge more than $500 on the secured card, the transaction simply won't go through.

- Get a retailer credit card. Another type of "training wheel" credit card is a card issued by a retail store or a gas company. In general, retail credit cards are easier to obtain than regular unsecured cards. The downside is that they don't carry as much weight on a credit report as a normal credit card. Beware: These types of cards tend to carry high interest rates.

- Apply for a small loan. Loans are a different kind of credit than credit cards. A loan is what's known as installment credit, since you pay back the loan, with interest, in set monthly installments. A mortgage, student loan or a car loan is a good example of installment credit. If you want to make a major purchase someday, it's a good idea to show lenders that you have some positive experience with installment credit. For many young borrowers, a student loan is a great way to begin using installment credit. Student loans carry relatively low interest rates and are reasonably easy to obtain. The best part about a student loan is that you don't have to start repaying the loan until six months after you graduate. The downside is that the loan won't appear on your credit report until you start paying it back.
- A good credit score will help you get loans for a home, car, and other big items. The interest rate you obtain for your loans will be based on your credit score.
- Get a good job and keep it. On every credit report, there's a section called "identifying information." In that section is a place to record employment history. One reason for including employment history on a credit report is to give hiring managers an easy way to verify information on a job application. Another reason is to give lenders subtle information about the character of a borrower.

Investing:
- *Before you have the money*, talk to an Investment Counselor or Financial Advisor.
- Find someone who wants to work with a young investor. Call around. Investigate before you invest. Study companies to learn what makes them successful.
- Be flexible and open-minded about types of investments.
- Don't just depend on someone else to invest your money. Read about investing and learn the basics. Read your investment statements. If you don't understand how to interpret the statement, get help. This is money for your future.
- Diversify. No matter how careful you are, you can neither predict nor control the future.

- Find out how often you can change your percentage of investments.
- Invest for maximum total real return. This means the return on invested dollars after taxes and after inflation.
- Don't panic. The market fluctuates. Learn from your mistakes. The basic rules of building wealth by investing in stocks will hold true. In this century or the next it's still "Buy low, sell high."

Retirement Accounts:

- Establish a retirement account now and contribute to it regularly.
- Treat your retirement fund like a regular monthly bill and don't miss a payment.
- Never withdraw from your retirement account. There are penalties for doing so.
- Take advantage of matching contributions from your employer.
- If you are self-employed, talk to an investment counselor.
- Know how your investment is doing. Check your quarterly statements. Change your investment percentages if you're not happy, but don't try to time the ups and downs.
- Do not count on Social Security benefits—they may not always be there.
- It is never too early or too late to start your nest egg, so start now.

Identify Theft

- Make photocopies of the front and back of every card you keep in your wallet. This includes Driver's License, debit/credit cards and insurance cards. Keep these copies safely at home as a record of all your account numbers, back-of-card security codes and contact information.
- If your wallet or purse goes missing, call your bank and credit card issuers. Make sure to tell them you want an "account number change." You do not need to close the account.
    - o File a report with your local police department. Get a copy of the report and send duplicates to your bank and credit-reporting bureaus.

o Place a fraud alert or security freeze on your file at the three major credit bureaus. (Experian, Equifax and TransUnion.)

o Contact your DMV for a replacement of your driver's license.

o Ask private medical and car/homeowners insurers for a replacement account number to avoid insurance fraud.

o Check your credit report about two weeks after the loss. Two weeks is enough time for thieves to apply for credit in your name, but generally not enough for new cards to be issued. Recheck your credit report two to three months later.

Chapter 16

On the Road Again

Have you done a lot of traveling? The rules and regulations change often, so always check with the airport, airline, train station, cruise ship, etc. on what their policy is. There is nothing more frustrating than having to throw away your toiletries because you didn't bring the correct size in your carry-on luggage. You need to know how far in advance you need to be at your travel station. Make sure to travel in comfortable clothing and wear shoes that are easy to slip on and off through the security checkpoints. Be aware of people who offer rides and are not driving commercial vehicles. It is best to arrange for a taxi in advance. If you travel overseas, make sure to bring some type of language interpreter. There are books, phone apps and hand held devices to help with this. When you get to your destination, make sure you know where to go and where not to go for your safety. Carry a map, which you can get online, or hard copy, or a global positioning system (GPS) to help you get to your destination.

Home Preparation:
- Unplug all appliances, except for the refrigerator.
- Set air conditioning thermostat up to 90 degrees. Set humidistat if applicable according to manufacturer's instructions.
- Arrange for mail pickup by a friend or neighbor, or put it on hold at the post office.

- Put a hold on your newspaper delivery (if applicable).
- Arrange for someone to mow your grass if you are going for an extended period of time. Tall grass is a sure sign that you are out of town.
- Clean out the refrigerator of anything that will expire while you are gone.
- Notify your alarm company (if applicable) that you will be out of town.
- Invest in a light control device or light timer. Plug one lamp into it, insert into the wall, and set the timer to turn the lamp on when it gets dark. You can also use the device on your Christmas tree lights.
- If you have a neighbor that can watch your house, that is great, but still use the light control timing device.
- If a neighbor watches your home or gets your mail, do something nice for him or her or bring them a souvenir from your trip.

Packing:
- When packing your suitcase, tightly roll up your clothes to make more room.
- Put your liquids in a plastic zippered bag in case they open.
- Pack one outfit for each day with one extra only. Many airlines charge for extra bags, so pack lightly. There is also a weight limit you have to meet to avoid paying extra.
- Make sure your suitcase zippers are in working order.
- Do not lock your suitcase. Many airport security personnel open bags to check them. They must have access to your suitcase.
- Do not put your travel itinerary in your suitcase.
- If you are going to take your suitcase on the airplane with you, check for the latest security requirements. It is best to purchase your toiletries at your destination.
- If your luggage gets lost, do not panic. Go to the airline customer service area and report the loss. They usually have extra toiletries to give you until your luggage arrives.
- If your luggage is permanently lost (yes, this happens), make sure to file a claim with the airline.

Car:

- Do not overload the car. This cuts down on gas mileage and creates wear/tear on your tires.
- Pack half of what you think you need. You know you always over pack!
- Keep your doors locked at all times.
- Keep windows clutter free. You need to be able to see out of every window.
- Fill up with gas when your tank reaches the ¼ mark. Do not wait for the low fuel indicator, as you may not be as close to a gas station as you think.
- Keep your windshield clean at all times.

Bills:

- If you are going to be gone for an extended period of time, write checks ahead and bring to mail. Mail at least seven days in advance of date due.
- Pay bills online: set the date of payment online at least 3 days in advance.

Hotels, Flights, Car Rental:

- Keep all documents in one place for easy access.
- Make sure you have your passport, if needed.
- Keep all credit card receipts to compare to the monthly statement.
- Sign up for the hotel and flight mileage clubs before you book. If you travel enough you will earn points for free stays and other travel freebies.
- Never book a premium hotel room or luxury car unless it's a very special occasion and you're worried about availability. Instead, save money by reserving a standard room or car and then asking for a free upgrade upon arrival. You can even get on-site upgrades on discounted rooms.

Paying for Your Trip:

- Do some pre-trip planning. Before traveling, consider subscribing to a daily deal website in your destination city. Websites like

Groupon, Living Social or Double Take Deals offer discounts at restaurants and attractions. You can easily access the vouchers from your mobile phone.

- It is best not to carry cash.
- If you must carry cash, make sure to split it up and store it in different places so that you do not carry it all with you at once in the event something is lost or stolen. Many hotels provide a safe in the room, so store your extra cash there.
- Save your spare change. Place all of your loose change in a jar and when you are ready to take a trip, cash it in. You will be surprised at how fast it all adds up.
- Make sure you know where your credits cards are at all times. Do not let them out of your sight. This is one of the ways identity theft happens.
- If you cannot afford to take a long trip, look for alternatives. Many people take a "stay-cation" (stay-at-home vacation) and still have a great time. When was the last time you explored the area where you live?

Chapter 17

Buying a Home/Renting an Apartment

Whether you are buying or renting, there is nothing more exciting than getting your first place. But there is a lot to do in preparation for this. It can be a really frustrating process, but just know in the end that it is worth the effort. Of all of the homes that I have owned, each one has a special place in my heart. Some caused great heartache in the purchase, but being a homeowner is a great feeling.

I never realized how much work buying or renting a home could be. There were so many deposits that I didn't budget for. I had no idea of the amount of money that it took for closing costs. It is very important to make sure you understand what will be involved before making the decision to move out of your parents' home.

Lastly, whether buying or renting, keep your yard and the outside of your home maintained. Nothing brings down the neighborhood more than overgrown shrubs and grass. House paint does not last forever. I am a licensed real estate sales associate, so I hope the information below will be helpful to you.

Deposits/Fees:
- Electric
- Water/sewer

- Phone
- Cable
- Trash/recycling
- For renting: usually first month of rent, last month of rent, and a security deposit
- Application fee for community neighborhoods or for renting.

Buying a Home:

- If you are moving to a new area, always rent before you buy, if you can. Get to know the areas of the town to see which fits you and/or your family best.
- If you're purchasing directly through the homeowner, make sure to have a real estate attorney review the contract.
- If purchasing through a realtor, take your time and do not get pressured to buy. You can still have a real estate attorney review the contract if you are unsure of the wording.
- Do not buy the first home you see. View several homes before deciding.
- Know what you can afford. Get pre-approved.
- Check out the neighborhood where you intend to buy.
- If you do not have children but plan to, check out the local schools where you intend to buy.
- Know where the nearest fire station is located. This could help lower the price of your homeowners insurance.
- Do not buy to the limit of what you "qualify" for. This will help you in the long run to prepare for life's unexpected events such as a loss of job or extended illness.
- Understand what you are signing. If you have questions and do not feel they are being answered, *do not sign.*
- Know when garbage pickup day is.
- Know when recycling day is.
- Find out if the property is in a flood zone. Shop around for quotes on flood insurance.
- Shop around for your homeowners insurance. Make sure you understand the policy and what it covers. Know what the policy will cover in the event of a natural disaster. Make sure you have

adequate coverage to rebuild your home in case disaster strikes. Be sure to get replacement coverage on your home and its contents.

- If you are part of a homeowners association, know the rules and abide by them.
- If there is a homeowners association, make sure to get in the application and fee in plenty of time before the closing.
- Get an estimated list of the closing costs so that you understand completely what funds you will need. You need to understand that this is an "estimated" listing and you will need to be prepared to pay more than the list states in some cases.
- If you do not have enough for a down payment, consider asking a relative for the money. They can give it as a gift and write it off on their taxes.

Renting:
- Make sure you understand the rental agreement. If you have questions, ask. If you do not understand, *do not sign.*
- Make sure to ask if there are any other charges that you will incur besides monthly rent.
- Know what utilities (if any) are included in your monthly rent (water, sewer, cable, garbage pickup.)
- Make sure you understand what is expected of the landlord and what is expected of you. For example: Which party is responsible for fixing broken items?
- Know when the landlord may access the property. Have set guidelines that you are comfortable with.
- Know when garbage pickup day is.
- Know when recycling day is.
- Check out the neighborhood where you intend to rent.
- If you do not have children but plan to, check out the local schools where you intend to rent.
- Shop around for your renters insurance and yes, get renters insurance. Know what the policy covers. (Natural Disasters)
- Ask your landlord if there is a homeowners association. If so, get a list of the rules and regulations and abide by them.

Moving:

- Change your mailing address through the post office at least a week before the move (if possible).
- Contact bank, loan, insurance company, credit card companies, and any other creditors with your change of address as soon as you know the new address.
- Send out change of address cards to family and friends.
- Ask family and friends to help you move. Provide food and drink.
- Take rest breaks during the move.
- Packing and moving is hard work, so be gentle and patient with those helping you.
- You do not have to unload all of those boxes in one day. They are not going anywhere and you need time to think about the best place to put your belongings.

Chapter 18

General Home Repair

Now that you have your home or apartment, you need to know the basics of home repair. The value of a home can change largely over time. Homes that are maintained well retain and even gain value, while those that are ignored can depreciate in terms of their overall worth. You can complete many different maintenance tasks around the house without costly professional assistance.

Hanging Pictures:
- To hang a picture properly, you want the center of the picture to be equal with the height of your eyes (adult eye height). Take time to measure correctly before you hammer in that nail.
- Plan where you want to hang your pictures and wall hangings. If your pictures are heavy (over 25 lbs.) it's best to position them over a wall stud. However, if you have a number of pictures they can't all be positioned on top of studs, so use plastic wall plugs.
- Figure out where studs are located in your walls. Use an electric stud finder, which is available at most hardware stores, or simply tap lightly on the wall with a hammer. Most of the wall will give off a hollow sound, but when you are tapping over a stud, the wall will sound much more solid.
- Determine the proper hanger for your wall. If you are hanging a relatively light picture (up to 25 lbs.) on drywall, you will prob-

ably just need a nail and a picture hanger. However, if you're hanging a heavier object you might want to consider using a plastic wall anchor or even a Molly bolt in the drywall. If your walls are concrete you can use a concrete plug fastened into the wall to hang your picture.

- Calculate the proper height to hang your picture by having someone hold a tape measure vertically up to your wall from floor to ceiling. Make a small mark on the wall equal to the height of your eyes about 55 inches.
- Measure the height of the picture to calculate the mid-point. For example, if your picture is 15 inches high, the mid-point is 7 ½ inches from the bottom or top. This midway point is called the centerline.
- Stretch the wire hanger on the back of your picture out (as if the picture was hanging on the wall) and measure from the centerline to the highest point of the wire (let's say it's 4 inches).
- Drive a nail into the mark (through your picture hanger) or install your wall anchors and carefully place your picture on it.
- Stand back to see if the picture is level. You can adjust this by sliding the picture left or right until it is level.

Squeaky Hinges:

- A squeaky door hinge can provide atmosphere around Halloween, but most of the time it's just annoying. Most squeaky hinges can be fixed by spraying on a small amount of water-displacing spray such as cooking spray. If that doesn't work, position a screwdriver beneath the hinge's pin and tap it with a hammer. The pin will separate from the barrel, allowing it to be pulled free. Scrub both the pin and barrel with steel wool, lubricate everything and then slide the pin back in place.

Tighten Loose Screws:

- Often times if a screw is removed and then re-inserted into its hole, it may not fit properly. This is because the hole has been stripped, preventing the threads on the screw from biting in properly. Before you insert the screw, poke a piece of toothpick into the hole. The extra material will put enough pressure onto the screw to allow it to grab the sides of the hole tightly.

Leaky Faucet:

- No matter how many times you try to tighten the faucet the leak won't stop. Tired of seeing your money trickle down the drain? A leaky faucet will cause your water bill to be higher than usual, so take the time to fix it. With just around five dollars and fifteen minutes, you can fix your own leaky faucet.

- First, you need to find out which line (hot or cold) is causing the leak. This is easy, just look under the sink for the main cut off knobs. Twist one of the knobs clockwise for off. Next, turn on water to drain any leftover in the pipe and shut back off. See if it has stopped. If not, test again using the other line (hot or cold) by shutting it off by turning the knob clockwise.

- By now you'll know whether it's the hot or cold water knob which is causing the problem. Make a mental note of which one and shut off both main lines under the sink.

- Next, on the knobs there is usually a plastic tab on the top. It's usually labeled either H for hot or C for cold. There are of course some variations. Using a flat headed screw driver, a small one, that can be easily pressed into the side of the plastic and easily pry it off. It should not be hard at all. They're just stuck in there like the top of a milk container.

- After that you should see a screw that needs to be taken out. Using the correct size screw driver, unscrew the screw by turning it counter-clockwise. This will undo the screw. Note that sometimes they can be rusty due to water condensation building up over the years. Just be careful as to not "strip" the screw, which means tear it up where a screw driver can no longer be used. When this happens, you have to use a drill and drill it out by cutting the metal. It's a real hassle so hopefully that won't happen. Just keep in mind that if it is, or if the screw gets stripped, it is not the end of the world. Just means you'll have to buy another screw and waste a good extra 5 minutes getting it out. If unable to remove, contact a professional plumber.

- Once that is complete you'll be able to remove the handle. Underneath the handle will be a metal fixture that can be simply pulled out or removed with a screwdriver. (Counter clockwise to remove something). Once that is complete you'll see at the bottom of this piece a rubber washer. It's a round seal; this is what keeps the water out. Most likely you'll notice that it is ripped, torn, and in some rare cases, completely gone. You want to remove this washer.
- Now, make a quick trip to the hardware store and find a washer that is the same size. If your washer is too badly damaged, just take the piece that the washer went into and then try out washers at the store. Also some market stores, such as the super grocery stores and other mainstream shopping places will have kits that contain an assorted variety of washers in a package for around three dollars.
- After you get your washer and return home, place the washer back into the fixture and put it all back together. Turn on the main lines once again slowly to make sure that you didn't leave anything undone and which would cause a leak and test it.

Clearing and Preventing Clogs:
- Do not use chemicals to clear clogged drains as they can actually erode cast-iron drain pipes. Use a plumber's snake. This can be purchased at your local hardware store.
- Start with vinegar and baking soda as this can clear most clogs quickly and economically.
- For best results follow the directions on the plumber snake package.
- To verify you have removed the clog, run the water for at least 2–5 minutes to test.
- Keep food scraps out of kitchen drains. Scrape food into the trash before doing dishes—even if you have a disposal—and never put liquid grease down the drain. Allow grease to cool and pour into a sealable container to put into the garbage.
- Keep hair out of the bathroom drains. Install screens over the drains in showers and tubs and pull out the hair daily after you bathe.

- Do not flush anything down the toilet other than sewage and toilet paper.

Stopping a leaky or running toilet:

- Leak finder – pour a packet of grape Kool-Aid in the tank of your toilet. If the water in the toilet bowl turns purple without flushing, your toilet is slowly leaking water – and money – down the drain. Installing a new flap or seal usually fixes it.
- Check the guide or chain on the tank stopper. If the rod is bent or the chain lines are twisted, just straighten them out.
- Take a look at the float mechanism. If lifting the ball up stops the water from running, try bending the float arm down to attain the right buoyancy. If the ball has water in it, it needs to be replaced. Unscrew it from the arm and put a new one in its place.
- If the toilet continues to run, the valve seat and stopper may have corrosion or build up preventing the stopper from closing. Lift the stopper up and check for any objects or substance that might prevent a tight seal. Gently scour the seat and the rim. If there is a great deal of damage or corrosion, replace the stopper and valve seat.
- The flush valve assembly may have to be replaced if the toilet is still running. Take the old parts with you when purchasing a new inside gasket and assembly to ensure a perfect match. If the shaft of the assembly is cracked, the shaft and assembly will need to be replaced. Again, take the flush valve assembly with you to the hardware store to get a perfect match.
- Keep in mind that the new replacement parts for toilets are easier to mount, set, and use. This might be better than replacing part by part. This may also provide a less expensive alternative to replacing parts. You need to decide which would be best for your situation.

Retrieving an item dropped down the drain:

- Turn off the water immediately to prevent the item from being washed away from reach.

- Open the cabinet below the sink.
- Find the P-trap, which is the U-shaped piece of pipe that connects the vertical pipe running from the sink to the horizontal pipe that goes into the wall.
- Place a bucket under the trap.
- With a large wrench, (plumber's pipe wrench or long nose pliers –purchase from local hardware store), loosen the large threaded nuts that attach the trap to the other pipes. Sometimes you can do this with your hands.
- Pull the trap off with a good yank, letting it fall into the bucket as necessary. The trap will be full of dirty water.
- Put on gloves. Empty the trap into your hand - over the bucket - and look for your valuable.
- Reassemble the P-trap, being careful not to over tighten the threaded nuts.
- Run the water and check for leaks.

Insulation:

- To avoid getting high utility bills, it is important to make sure your home is kept properly insulated all year. In the winter, quality insulation can prevent cold air from making its way inside. Check all the doors in windows in a home to make sure extra air is not seeping through. Storm doors are a good way to protect against the outside elements. Additionally, check all of the frames surrounding windows and doors for weak spots, cracks and holes that may be letting in air or precipitation. Install insulation for all pipes in the attic to make sure they are protected from cold weather. Ensure that the roof is insulated well so that inside temperatures do not get excessively cold in the winter or warm during the summer.

Roof:

- Check on the status of your roof by inspecting it with a ladder or binoculars. If there are missing shingles or breaks, repair them using shingles and roofing cement. If your roof needs to be replaced, contact a roofing company. A roof in poor shape can deteriorate under harsh precipitation during winter, resulting in leaks and loss of warm air.

Gutters:

- Remove leaves and other debris from gutters. If gutters are blocked, excessive rain, snow and ice can build up and may break the gutter or damage the roof.

Painting:

- Examine your home inside and out, fence, shed and any other outdoor structures to see whether they need repainting. Work to restore paint while weather is cool and dry so that the paint cures properly. Cracking paint on a home, deck or shed exposes the material below the paint. This can cause permanent damage if the material is exposed to a wet, cold winter.
- Preparation is one of the key elements to a good paint job. Paint requires a clean, smooth surface to spread evenly and stick well. Clean all the walls you plan to paint before starting your paint job, and use a paint scraper to remove paint chips. Sand down pronounced edges where large paint chips are removed, but be sure to remove sandpaper filings with a tack cloth or dust rag before painting. If there are large gouges in the surface, fill them in with spackle or stucco before applying paint.
- When you are ready to paint, use drop cloths to cover all the surfaces in the room that are not going to be painted. Apply painter's tape along edges and corners. Meticulous taping can help prevent accidentally painting on the wrong surface, and it makes painting along corners and molding easier.
- The proper way to apply paint and the conditions necessary for drying can vary from one type of paint to another. Always read and follow the instructions on the paint can. Take note of how much area the paint is meant to cover and compare that to the area of the surfaces you plan to paint. If the paint has harmful fumes, work in a well-ventilated room and consider using fans and a mask to help protect you from fumes.

- Use long, vertical strokes when painting with a brush. Horizontal strokes are more likely to result in running paint and are more difficult to control. If you are using a paint roller, roll it in paint and then roll it up and down a few times on the sloped part of the paint pan to roll off excess paint. Paint a "W" shape with the roller, moving horizontally along the wall, and then fill in the "W" with the rest of the paint on the roller. Apply more paint to the roller and work your way horizontally across the wall in this manner. When you are finished painting, refer to the paint can for brush cleaning instructions. Latex paint can be removed with water, while oil-based paints require paint thinner or other solvents.

Making windows airtight:

- Remove old caulk, paint chips and dirt from around windows.
- Cut ¼ inch from the top of the caulking tube with a utility knife.
- Slide tube into caulking gun. If you prefer there are tubes that you can squeeze instead of using a caulking gun. Check your hardware store for options.
- Squeeze 1/8 inch of caulk between window frame and siding. Look for any signs that the elements can get into your home.
- Smooth the edge of the caulk with an ice cream stick. Clean the excess on the stick about every six inches.
- Let dry about 24 hours before painting.
- Tight on a budget? Insulate odd-shaped and out-of-the-way windows by cutting a piece of bubble wrap to fit the window, and then spray the inside of the window with a little water. Apply the bubble wrap with the bubble side on the glass. It will cling to the glass for weeks and comes off easily.

Air Conditioner/Heater/Furnace/Fireplace:

- Have your air conditioner and/or furnace serviced once a year.
- If you see that you have any type of heating/cooling system leak, contact a professional immediately.
- If you smell gas and are able to turn the gas valve off then do so, otherwise leave the home and call a professional immediately.

- Have an efficiency review of your heating/cooling systems once every 5 years.
- Do not store anything in front of the air conditioner vent (where large filter is).
- Keep heating and cooling vents clean and free from furniture and draperies.
- Your heating system will be frequently used in the cold winter months. Schedule yearly maintenance before cold weather begins. Inspect and change filters as directed.

Chapter 19

Car Buying Basics

I have a lot of experience in buying cars. I believe I have purchased over sixteen cars in my lifetime so far. With the purchase of each car, I have learned more and more. I believe that car buying is an art. It takes a lot of focus to get around the sales pitches and separate fact from fiction. I create a spreadsheet to compare vehicles. I carry this spreadsheet with me so that the sales people know I did my homework. I do have respect for people trying to do the best job they can, but it really does not take five people to sell a car. A good deal should only involve one sales person and the approval of the manager on site. Do not be fooled into believing that they are giving you a fantastic deal that no one else gets. Do not get me wrong—I love my salesperson friends; I just want you to be on your toes when it comes to making a large purchase, whether it is a car, boat, or other type of vehicle. Remember the car you buy does not define you. You just need reliable transportation.

Before You Buy:
- Do your homework and create a spreadsheet on the different cars that interest you. This should include the features important to you for your purchase.
- Be open to new and used vehicles.
- Check the car rating sites and insurance sites for information about testing done on the vehicle, especially crash testing.

- Know what you can afford.
- Know the different financing options available to you.
- Get your financing ahead of time. Make sure to provide the necessary financial papers to your lending institution in a timely manner.
- Determine if you want to buy or lease the vehicle.
- Do not lease if you intend to put a lot of miles on the vehicle.
- Make a list of questions to ask the salesperson.
- Contact your insurance company to see what your rate would be on the specific car you are interested in.

During the Purchase:

- Do not be intimidated and/or pressured to buy anything.
- Do not purchase the first day you look.
- Make sure to test drive the vehicle.
- Make sure there is plenty of leg room in both front and back.
- Make sure there is ample head room, especially if you or your spouse is tall.
- Know what incentives are available to you.
- Ask to see the invoice.
- Negotiate the price. You do not have to pay sticker price.
- Ask what the dealership offers that is included in pricing. Are oil changes or any other maintenance included?
- When you are shopping for a used car, check the oil on the dipstick. If the oil is thick, dark or sludgy, then this car has not been maintained and should be avoided.
- Do not include maintenance in the financing.
- Do not finance longer than forty-eight months unless you intend to keep the vehicle for the life of the loan. Once you leave the lot with the car, the car begins to depreciate. If you finance for longer than forty-eight months and want to trade after a few years, your payoff will be more than the worth of the vehicle, therefore you could create a state of being "up-side down" in the vehicle. The term "up-side down" means that you owe more than the vehicle is worth.

- If you purchase a used vehicle from a dealership, make sure to ask for a history of the vehicle. They can print this for you. There are companies that provide this online.
- If you purchase a used vehicle from a private party, then ask to see the receipts from the maintenance records. You can also go online and print your own car history for a small fee.
- If you do not know a lot about cars, bring someone with you who does. Have someone look the used vehicle over before you purchase.
- Make sure to purchase Guaranteed Auto Protection (GAP) insurance. This insurance covers you in the event your car is totaled and your car insurance does not cover the entire loss of the car.
- Understand your warranty.
- Do not sign a contract if you do not understand it.
- There is no return policy on the car if you are not completely satisfied, so make sure you are completely satisfied with the deal.
- If you don't feel comfortable or it doesn't "feel right," simply walk away.

After the Purchase:
- Make sure that you understand how to fully operate the vehicle before leaving the lot or home of the person from whom you purchased the car.
- Make sure you get everything promised to you in writing with a date of when you will receive it.
- Have vehicle maintenance performed regularly as instructed by the owners' manual or dealership.

Chapter 20

Car Care Tips

You saved to purchase the car you wanted, so make sure you keep it maintained. We need to treat a car like we would treat ourselves; with plenty of attention and care. Take some time now to look at the manual. If you purchased a used car and it didn't come with a manual, you can usually purchase one at the local auto parts store. Maintenance such as oil changes, maintaining fluid levels, checking tire pressure, or changing your windshield wiper blades you can do on your own. If you do prefer to do your own oil changes, make sure to properly dispose of the old oil. You can save money doing your own car maintenance. You know how much mechanics charge to change your oil, so if you can do it yourself, then you will have extra money for other things in your budget. If you think about it, you could save hundreds of dollars a year just doing the work yourself. There is nothing wrong with taking your car to a mechanic, but do your homework beforehand. Make sure you know in advance what they charge and be sure that they offer you an agreement not to go over a certain dollar amount without contacting you first.

General Maintenance:
- Keep a log of the maintenance done on your car.
- Change oil every 3000 to 5000 miles or per dealership recommendations. This is so important because if the oil becomes dirty, the engine will not be able to run properly and

will eventually begin to burn the oil that it does have. This shortens the life of your engine drastically.

- Keep fluid levels maintained at optimal levels. Fluids such as such as transmission oil, power-steering fluid, antifreeze and window washer fluid.
- Change windshield wipers once a year when rainy season starts.
- Have tune ups according to your users' manual. Check with the dealership or mechanic to see what is included in a tune up. You may be able to do some of this work yourself. It is not recommended that you change your timing belt, since most engines must be taken apart to do so. Some cars do not have timing belts, they have timing chains. The average time to have this changed is around 60,000 to 100,000 miles.

Oil Change:

Supplies needed:
- A socket/spanner to undo the plug
- Oil filter clamp
- New Oil – Use oil recommended by manufacturer.
- New filter – Use filter as recommended by manufacturer.
- Tray to empty oil in. This cannot be discarded in your personal garbage. It will need to be dropped off at a station that takes oil. Many places will take your used motor oil for free or find someone that uses a waste oil heater during the winter months. They will happily take any oil you have that does not have water or other contaminants in it.
- Funnel to pour in new oil

Changing the oil:
- Place the tray under the oil pan - where you intend to empty it. (under the car)
- Use the socket to undo the oil pan bolt.
- Allow ample time for the oil to drain.
- Seal up the sump plug – This is a very important piece. If you don't have this in place, the new oil you pour will go straight through to the ground.

- Insert the funnel into the oil reservoir and refill the oil.
- You also want to check the air filter while changing the oil. This needs to be replaced at least once a year and is inexpensive.
- Make sure to dispose of the oil properly.
- If you spill any oil it can easily be soaked up with oil dry or kitty litter.

Changing Spark Plugs:

- This may be done once a year. However many new cars come with 100,000 mile plugs. Check your manual for guidelines on replacing.
- To replace a spark plug, there are certain sockets that fit into your socket wrench. You need to unscrew the rocker cover that covers over your engine.
- You will then unscrew the spark plug and pull it out.
- If the connection looks burnout or white, then you need to change it. One thing to be very careful of when you are replacing a spark plug is to get it back in straight without hitting the tip on anything.
- If your spark plugs have oil all over it, then you need to show your mechanic, there may be something wrong with your car that he will be able to identify.

Coolant Changes:

- This needs to be a part of your maintenance schedule and should be done once a year. The coolant prevents your car from overheating. Ever see a car on the side of the road with the hood up and lots of steam coming from the engine? Well, they are overheating.
- Changing your radiator fluid can easily prevent this. You will do this by unhooking the hose and let what fluid is there drain out. You will need a BIG bucket and a place to dispose of the fluid. Reconnect the hose and make sure it is connected well, where it won't leak.
- Refill your radiator with coolant to the fill line.

- Replace cap. It's that easy and can save you so much money. Check the price of a radiator flush the next time you are at the auto mechanics. It is not cheap.

Tires:

- Your tires should be regularly inspected for wear and punctures.
- Tires should be replaced every 2–3 years, depending on tire type and the surfaces you drive on.
- Rotate tires every 5000 to 7000 miles or per dealership recommendations.
- Check your owners' manual or look in the side of the door to see what the recommended tire pressure is for the front and rear tires. It can be different for both. Under inflation causes tire wear and wastes fuel.
- Keep all wheels in proper alignment. Improper alignment not only causes faster tire wear but also puts an extra load on the engine.

Other Car Care Tips:

- Do not carry excess weight in your vehicle. Excess weight puts a heavier load on the engine, causing greater fuel consumption.
- Accelerate slowly and smoothly. Avoid jackrabbit starts. Get into a higher gear as quickly as possible.
- Avoid long engine idling. If you have to wait for a long period of time, it is better to turn off the engine and start again later.
- Avoid engine lag or over-revving. Use a gear position suitable for the type of road you're traveling.
- Avoid stop-and-go driving. Stop-and-go driving wastes fuel.
- Do not rest your foot on the clutch or brake pedal. This causes needless wear, overheating and poor fuel economy.
- Keep a safety kit in your car at all times.

Chapter 21

Be Computer Smart

Since just about every household has a computer of some kind today, I am sure you are already familiar with the information below. This is basic information, but it will benefit you in the long run. Computers are expensive, so you need to take good care of them so that they last a long time. I cannot stress how important it is to have a good spyware and anti-virus program. If you get any type of virus, they can completely erase your hard drive and all of your information will be gone. If your computer isn't properly protected, someone could hack into it and steal personal information you may have stored there. Do not make yourself vulnerable to these attacks.

Computer Basics:
- Use a good surge protector.
- Unplug electrical equipment during a lightning storm. Even the best surge protector cannot block a lightning strike.
- Do not click on e-mail attachments that you are not expecting and you do not know the sender.
- Do not fall for phishing schemes. You are not going to get rich quick and that person from Nigeria is not really going to send you millions.
- When you have a computer problem, look for the obvious first. Always make sure the device is plugged in and all cables are attached.

- When all else fails, restart the system.
- If the power goes off, unplug the system. When power is restored, there are surges and spikes that can damage your equipment. Plug it back in after the power is restored.
- To clean the keyboard, turn the system off, turn the keyboard upside down and shake to remove crumbs. You can use a spray device from a computer store.
- Wipe the dust gently from the screen. Do not press hard on a laptop screen, as it can cause permanent damage.
- Do not give personal information to anyone in a chat room.
- Limit the personal information that you provide on social sites.
- If you are going to use the Internet for dating, use reputable Web sites, not chat rooms.
- Make sure to set your security settings on your social sites. Do not let just anyone view your information.
- If you use a wireless router, make sure to password protect it. If you do not do this, your neighbor can use your wireless and possibly hack into your computer.
- If you use Wi-Fi at a local coffee house or restaurant, make sure you shield the laptop screen from the wandering eyes around you.
- Install a good spyware and antivirus software program to protect your computer from hackers.
- When purchasing something online, only put in personal information on Web sites that are trusted and locked. You will see a padlock somewhere on the site that will indicate that they are safe.
- When all else fails, contact customer support for your product.

Buying a New/Used Computer:
- I strongly suggest that you do not purchase a used computer. Although there are many rebuilt systems out there that would probably suit your needs, many of them have hidden problems. These problems are just waiting to surface. I feel the same about printers.
- Know what you can afford.

- Decide if you want a desktop computer or a laptop. Unless you need super speed or something special, a laptop will satisfy 90% of what most people need. Laptops are more portable, take up less space, and work just as well.
- Check the clearance aisle at the local office supply store or electronic store. These computers are still new and you can get a good deal. Most times you can save one hundred to two hundred dollars.
- I highly recommend a wireless router, especially if you purchase a laptop. You can use the laptop anywhere in your home. Do not forget to password protect it.
- Buy a new system with a reputable brand name and get a good warranty.
- Know if the price includes a warranty for support, or if that is an additional cost.
- Create a spreadsheet of the systems that you are interested in. It will help to point out the features you really want and could be missing from other systems.
- Determine what software you want included in the purchase and what you will buy later.
- Do not buy something that is more powerful than what you really need. Knowing the hardware you need is very important.
- If you do not know a lot about computers, speak to someone who does, such as a friend, relative, coworker (not the salesperson), especially about the hardware.
- If you buy a laptop, invest in a comfortable carry case.
- If you buy a laptop, invest in an extra battery especially if you travel a lot.
- If you buy a desktop computer, make sure you have plenty of room for a desk and the printer.

Chapter 22

Taking Care of Yourself

Most of my lifetime has been spent trying to please and take care of others. I never realized that if I did not take good care of myself, I would not be able to take care of my family. Taking time out to do something for yourself does not make you a selfish person, regardless of what others say. You have to have peace of mind to concentrate on the tasks at hand. If you are overwhelmed and do not take a time out, your work and family life could suffer. You do not have to spend a lot of money to have time to yourself. Reading a magazine on the patio away from everyone works well. Go for a walk. Take a bubble bath. Just make sure to allow the same courtesy to your partner. He (or she) needs time too.

Me, Myself, and I:
- Although it is very important to devote time to your relationship, time for yourself is just as important.
- Take care of yourself first and everything else will fall into place. If you are not well, you cannot take care of others.
- The old saying "if mom is not happy, no one is happy" is pretty much true! So take time for you.
- Be true to yourself.
- Love yourself. Love yourself. Love yourself.
- Be yourself no matter where you are.

- Be confident in everything you do.
- There is no shame in getting professional help if you feel overwhelmed or depressed.
- Your car, home, and job do not define you. You define you.
- Get a manicure, pedicure, or massage when time and your budget permits. Or, get together with a friend and give each other a manicure or pedicure.
- Get your yearly medical exams and blood work done.
- For women: do self-breast exams once a month. Ask your doctor to show you how.
- For males: do testicular exams once a month. Ask your doctor to show you how.
- When you get stressed out, ask yourself if it will matter in five years. If the answer is no, let it go. If it is yes, find a solution.

Character Traits

What character traits do you want to possess? Good personal character traits will better your chances of success in achieving your goals in both your personal life and your business life. Good social character traits result in other people wanting to do business with you or to have personal relationships with you.

Below are some personal trait guidelines:
- Temperance – Avoid excessive food and drink.
- Order – Organize your time effectively and keep all things in their place.
- Resolution – Do what you resolve to do without fail.
- Frugality – Spend only what benefits yourself and others and waste nothing.
- Moderation – Avoid extremes and forgive injuries. Injuries refers to an injury caused by another, whether physical or emotional—don't indulge your resentment.
- Industry – Be diligent and use your time productively.
- Cleanliness – Tolerate no uncleanliness in body, clothes, or home.

- Tranquility – Don't sweat the small stuff. And, it's all small stuff.
- Humility – Imitate Jesus and Socrates.
- Sincerity – Be fair in thought and word.
- Silence – Speak only to benefit yourself and others.
- Justice – Do no harm and do your duty.
- Chastity – Keep your lust in check.
- Morals & Values – Establish the morals and values of how you want to live your life. Associate with those that share these and remove yourself from the company of those that don't.

We must consider those genetic traits, such as eating disorders and drinking alcohol in excess, which may pose difficulty in the temperance guideline. However, it does not mean a person fails to follow the above guidelines. After all, no one is perfect.

Chapter 23

Love the One You're With

After my first marriage, I really did not think that there would be another person for me. Fortunately I was wrong, and I learned that just because one relationship does not work doesn't mean another one won't. Both parties have to be present and willing to make the relationship work. A relationship cannot be one-sided. Unfortunately, a divorce is pretty easy to get and marriage seems to be taken lightly in today's society. Marriage is meant to be forever, so make sure that you love the one you're with. I learned most of the advice I offer below the hard way, and I hope that you can learn from my mistakes.

Relationship Basics:
- Relationships are important—do not take them lightly. Relationships need constant repair and nurture. Neglected relationships make it tough to stand the test of time.
- Each person is responsible for giving 80 percent to make the relationship work. If you only have each person giving 50 percent, it will not work. You have to give the extra to show you really care. Relationships build and are nourished only when it is positively beneficial to both parties.
- No one is always right. It takes a big person to admit mistakes. Admit them and move on.

- Opposites do attract. You will not always be in sync with everything the other person wants to do. You must be willing to compromise.
- When you get angry, make sure to talk it out that day. Do not hold on to the past, especially during future arguments.
- Do not criticize—*no one* is perfect.
- Communicate often and openly.
- Do not suffocate each other. Time away is not a bad thing. Absence does make the heart grow fonder!
- Trust is *everything*. If you do not trust your partner, you will not be happy.
- Pay bills together so that each person knows the financial situation.
- Discuss and agree upon large purchases such as cars, homes, and boats.
- Never go to bed angry.
- Always kiss and hug before leaving your partner—it may be the last time you see him.
- Relationships that are true and positive should be sincere, natural, and voluntary. Real relationships are not forced.
- Be an example to your children. They pick up everything. This includes both cross words and loving words.
- Forget the drama and focus on being happy.
- Spend time with other happy couples.
- Keep your computer time to a minimum while with your partner. Use the computer after your spend quality time together.
- If you have children, take one night a week away from the kids. Work out a swap with other couples with children or find a good babysitter, preferably one who is certified in CPR.
- It is okay to have a girls' night out, just allow the same courtesy to your partner.
- Go to church together. A happy family is one that not only stays together, but prays together.
- Do not keep secrets that you know could cause major issues. They will eventually come out.

- If you feel the need to cheat on your spouse, talk to him and see what is missing in your relationship. Ask yourself if it is really worth losing everything you worked so hard to build.
- Give each other massages, manicures, and/or pedicures.
- Sex is a very important part of the relationship, but it is not the entire relationship. Do not base your relationship totally on sex.

Chapter 24

Simple Etiquette

The information below should be a refresher to you. There is a lot more to etiquette and how to behave, but I believe I have covered the basics on what you will need to know in order not to embarrass yourself and others. Most of the information I was raised with, and the rest was found in my readings. You do not have to be rich or royalty to have manners.

Use Your Manners:
- Turn the cell phone and/or other handheld device off during a luncheon meeting, social function, a medical appointment, on public transportation, and where indicated by signage.
- Hold the door. Whether you're male or female, open a door that you have just passed through for the next person directly behind you.
- Say please and thank you to waiters, store clerks, and other service personnel. The little things go a long way.
- Hold drinks and/or food, briefcases, or files in your left hand, keeping your right hand free to shake hands.
- Always send a thank-you note after attending an event, receiving a gift, or receiving a favor.
- Make eye contact and offer a sincere smile in every situation.
- Be perceptive and survey a situation. Always use your best judgment.

- Do not burp without excusing yourself in public places.
- When someone sneezes, acknowledge it with a "Bless you" or what your culture deems appropriate.
- Do not cross your hands over your chest when talking with someone. It implies that you are blocking them and are not interested.
- Always give a proper greeting to show confidence and maturity (Mr., Mrs., Doctor, etc.).
- Do not interrupt someone when they are speaking. Wait for a break in the conversation.
- When dining with a large group, wait for the entire group to get their food served before eating, unless it's agreed upon by everyone that it is okay to begin eating.
- Always respond to an invitation within a week of receiving it.
- Dress according to the dress code (if any). Do not attempt to "out dress" the hostess.
- Make sure to call ahead of time if you are going to bring guests with you when you have been invited somewhere.
- Do not talk with your mouth full.
- Do not chew with your mouth open.
- Try to limit the "crunch" of those crunchy foods.
- Do not reach across other people to get something you need.
- Do not pick your teeth or lick your fingers.
- Walk on the right side and pass on the left on sidewalks and other walkways.
- Always give up your seat for an elderly or handicapped person.
- If you have been invited to a friends' home for dinner, make sure to bring something with you. A nice dish you like to prepare, a bottle of wine, chocolates, or flowers is appropriate.
- Do not play your stereo loud enough to vibrate things around you such as walls, cars, and windows.

Chapter 25

Gift-giving Ideas

Gifts, or presents, are something everyone likes to receive. I believe the thought behind the gift is the most important part. A gift does not have to be expensive to be a great gift. If you cannot afford to give a gift, at least give a card. A card denotes that you cared enough to acknowledge the occasion and took the time to go to the store to shop for it. Depending on the occasion, a phone call would be a nice gift. Just take time out of your busy day to acknowledge others. It will brighten the day of everyone involved. Keep the dates of these special occasions in a place that will remind you ahead of time. Use your phone calendar, desk calendar, computerized calendar, or wall calendar. Make sure to get the gifts and/or cards in the mail at least five to seven days ahead of the occasion.

Special Reasons and Occasions for Gifting:
- Love (Valentine's Day) or friendship
- Gratitude for a gift received
- Piety (in the form of charity)
- Solidarity (in the form of mutual aid)
- Wealth sharing
- Solace (to offset misfortune)
- Graduation (Kindergarten, High School, College)
- Travel, in the form of souvenirs
- Housewarming
- Christening/Baptism

- Birthday (most commonly for a family member, girlfriend, or boyfriend)
- Potlatch (in societies where status is associated with gift-giving rather than acquisition)
- Christmas (People give one another gifts, often supposedly receiving them from Santa Claus.)
- Saint Nicholas (People give one another gifts, often supposedly receiving them from Saint Nicholas.)
- Wedding
- Wedding anniversary
- Funeral (Visitors bring flowers; the relatives of the deceased give food or drinks after the ceremony.)
- Birth of a Child
- Passing an examination/Licensure
- Father's Day
- Mother's Day
- Exchange of gifts between a guest and a host (often a traditional practice)
- Sale (for example, a lagniappe, which is a small gift given to a customer by a merchant at the time of a purchase, such as a "buy three get one free" promotion).

Re-gifting or Re-giving

This is where you give a gift that you have received in the past to another person. Re-gifting has become popular with white elephant gift exchanges (a popular holiday party game). There are just a couple of important things to remember:
- Rewrap the gift.
- Do not use it before re-gifting it.
- Do not give it back to the original gift-giver.

Gift Ideas with Low Cost in Mind
- A photo in a nice frame.
- A donation to a charity in the name of the person receiving the gift.
- A gift card to a favorite place such as a restaurant, bookstore, hardware store. etc.

- Homemade coupons you can make with your computer. Good for babysitting, massages, house cleaning, car washing, etc.
- A personalized photo book. There are several online sites to make these, or you can order them in the photo department of your local drugstore or department store.
- Something from your local craft store—lots of ideas in there like wreaths, jewelry, and shirt decorations. Handmade items are greatly appreciated.
- Start a scrapbook for someone and allow them to finish.
- Music CD or Movie DVD
- Ornaments (Christmas or other hanging-type ornaments)
- A chocolate or candy basket.
- Fresh-cut flowers from the market.
- A bottle of wine.
- Chip in with other family members or friends to buy a gift.
- Make a nice meal for someone.
- Make a nice dessert such as cake, brownies, or cookies and place in a decorated tin that you can purchase from your local discount store.
- A card and call on the day of the occasion. Always a good idea if you live far away from the gift recipient.

If you are still unsure, ask them what they need or want; keep the guesswork out of it.

Wrapping the Gift

In many cultures, gifts are usually wrapped or packaged in some manner. For example, in Western culture, gifts are often wrapped in wrapping paper and usually accompanied by a gift note or card, which may note the occasion. In Chinese culture, red wrapping denotes luck. In Japanese culture, wrapping paper and boxes are common; however, the traditional cloth wrapping called *furoshiki* is increasing in popularity. Put in the special effort to find out what is customary in the gift recipient's culture. Giving a gift in the bag from the store at which you purchased it is unacceptable. Put some thought and effort into it.

- Choose wrapping paper for the occasion. Newspaper comics make good wrapping paper!

- Make sure to cut the paper straight.
- Use clear tape, not duct tape. Wrapping the entire gift in duct tape is not considered wrapping paper.
- Ribbon is a nice touch, but not necessary.
- A bow is even nicer, but not necessary.
- Take pride in your gift wrapping; how would you like to receive it?
- If you do not have wrapping paper, find a gift box or bag that fits the gift. Use tissue paper to conceal the gift.
- Always attach a card.

Anniversary Gift Table by Year

Anniversary #	Traditional Gift	Modern Gift
First	Paper	Clocks
Second	Cotton	China
Third	Leather	Crystal/Glass
Fourth	Fruit/Flowers	Appliances
Fifth	Wood	Silverware
Sixth	Candy/Iron	Wood
Seventh	Wood/Copper	Desk Set
Eighth	Bronze/Pottery	Linens/Lace
Ninth	Pottery/Willow	Leather
Tenth	Aluminum/Tin	Diamond Jewelry
Eleventh	Steel	Fashion Jewelry
Twelfth	Silk/Linen	Pearls
Thirteenth	Lace	Textiles/Fur
Fourteenth	Ivory	Gold Jewelry
Fifteenth	Crystal	Watches
Twentieth	China	Platinum
Twenty-fifth	Silver	Silver
Thirtieth	Pearl	Diamond
Thirty-fifth	Coral	Jade
Fortieth	Ruby	Ruby
Forty-fifth	Sapphire	Sapphire
Fiftieth	Gold	Gold
Fifty-fifth	Emerald	Emerald
Sixtieth	Diamond	Diamond

Chapter 26

Shopping Smart

There are the things you need and then things you want. And then there are the things you didn't even know you wanted, but you're out window shopping or shopping online, and now you see new things you haven't seen before. You're in grave danger of blowing your monthly budget on something you could probably live without. If you are going shopping just for fun, leave your money, checkbook and debit/credit cards at home.

Before you buy, ask yourself:
- Am I buying this just because it is on sale?
- Do I really want or need this item?
- Can I afford this product, even on sale?
- Do I want to buy it, even if it adds to my credit card debt?

Preparing for the purchase:
- Find free items. Many online retailers offer samples of products and online coupons and rebates.
- Register at online coupon websites. Print coupons just before going to the store.
- Thrift stores. Check out your local thrift stores. Many people donate new, unused items that you can get at a huge discount. Did you know Goodwill has an online auction site? You can bid on treasures from Goodwill thrift stores across the country.
- Don't forget the local garage sales and flea markets. Many used items still have plenty of life left in them.

- Why not pray for rain! Look for special sale items that are currently out of stock. Ask for a rain check so that you can pick them up later – at the sale price – when you really need them.
- When ordering over the phone, ask if there are any special promotions. Many times there are specials offered, including discounts for free shipping that the operator isn't allowed to mention unless the customer asks.
- Free shipping. Some sites offer free shipping with a minimum purchase. Watch for these free shipping days.
- Post-holiday bargains. Whether it's Halloween costumes or holiday decorations, many stores discount these items 50-90% after the holiday.
- Set an amount limit on gifts that your purchase for others and stick to it. For holiday gifts, start early and spread the purchases over several months to avoid using credit cards.
- Comparison shop. Take time to comparison shop online before going to the store. This can save on time and gas. There are many apps out there that will comparison shop for you. If you are already in the store, and have an app scanner on your phone, you can scan the bar code of an item and compare in-store and online prices at other retailers.

Shopping:

- Make a list and buy only those items you need.
- Only bring the cash you need for the item you intend to purchase.
- Don't shop when you're bored, tired or sad. Mood extremes may lead to unwise purchases.
- When in doubt, don't buy it. Leave the store.
- Pick your shopping friends wisely. Don't overspend just because they do.
- Before you buy it, ask yourself "Can I make this?"

After the purchase:

- If you or a friend has a truck, pick up large purchases yourself and save on delivery costs.

- Always save your receipts. You can still return the product with a receipt. This will come in handy if you see the item on sale after your purchase. You can return to the store and get the sale price.
- Keep all contracts, sales receipts, canceled checks, warranty documents and owner's manuals in the event you have an issue with your purchase. Keep for the life of the item.
- If you encounter a problem with your purchase, you can write a complaint letter to the seller to explain your problem and how you would like them to resolve it. If the seller will not help you or respond to your complaint, you should then contact the manufacturer. Continue this process of reporting the problem in writing to industry trade organizations, local consumer protection agencies, and if necessary the Better Business Bureau, until your problem is resolved.

People joke about "shopaholics," but true compulsive spending is a serious disease. While it is often a problem associated with women, there are no gender barriers to the condition. Look for warning signs:

- Are you buying things you never end up using?
- Do you spend more time trolling for deals than doing your homework, housework or hanging out with friends?
- Are your credit cards at their limits?

If any of these habits sound like you, you may have a shopping addiction. Get professional help before it gets out of hand.

Chapter 27

Disaster Preparedness

No matter what type of disaster, storm or weather alert you have in your area, there is some preparation you can do ahead of time. There are many types of disasters however I will discuss those encountered in most areas. Please note that many of the items are duplicated throughout the different disasters, especially the "after" items. However, I felt it pertinent to add to each section to avoid missing pertinent information for that particular disaster in your area.

Type of Disasters:

Chemical Emergencies	Dam Failure
Earthquake	Fire or Wildfire
Flood	Hazardous Material
Heat	Hurricane
Landslide	Nuclear Power Plant Emergency
Terrorism	Thunderstorm
Tornado	Tsunami
Volcano	Winter Storm

Make a Plan:

- Your family may not be together when disaster strikes. It is important to plan in advance: how you will contact one another; how you will get back together; and what you will do in different situations. Appoint one contact out of town that everyone can call to check in.
- Plan for your animals: store veterinary records online, along with a current photo of your pet in case you get separated.

- Depending on your situations and the nature of the emergency, the first important decision is whether you stay where you are or evacuate. You should understand and plan for both possibilities. Use common sense and available information, including what you are learning here, to determine if there is an immediate danger. In any emergency, local authorities may or may not immediately be able to provide information on what is happening and what you should do. However, you should watch TV, listen to the radio or check the Internet often for information or official instruction as it becomes available.
- Find out what kinds of disasters, both natural and man-made, are most likely to occur in your area and how you will be notified. Methods of getting your attention vary from community to community. One common method is to broadcast via emergency radio and TV broadcasts. You might hear a special siren, or get a telephone call, or emergency workers may go door-to-door.
- You may also want to inquire about emergency plans at places where your family spends time: work, daycare and school. If no plans exist, consider volunteering to help create one. Talk to your neighbors about how you can work together in the event of an emergency. You will be better prepared to safely reunite your family and loved ones during an emergency if you think ahead and communicate with others in advance.

Emergency Supply Kit:
- Have this ready to go at all times. Reevaluate every 6 months.
- Water, one gallon of water per person per day for at least three days, for drinking and sanitation or a quality water filter kit found in most camping or outdoor stores.
- Good Backpack
- Food, at least a three-day supply of non-perishable food.
- Battery-powered or hand crank radio and a NOAA Weather Radio with tone alert and extra batteries for both.
- Quality LED Flashlight and extra batteries or solar charger with rechargeable batteries work well.

- First Aid Kit with first aid manual or guide.
- Whistle to signal for help.
- Dust mask, to help filter contaminated air and plastic sheeting and duct tape to shelter-in-place.
- Rain gear
- Garbage bags, plastic ties and moist hand wipes for personal sanitation.
- Wrench or pliers to turn off utilities.
- Can opener for food.
- Local maps or a GPS (global positioning system) with solar charger.
- Cell phone with chargers, inverter or solar charger.
- Prescription medications, over the counter medications such as Aspirin, and glasses.
- Infant formula and diapers.
- Pet food, vet records and extra water for your pet.
- Important family documents such as copies of insurance policies, identification and bank account records in a waterproof, portable container.
- Cash and change - a roll or two of quarters only since change can be heavy.
- Sleeping bag or warm blanket for each person. Consider additional bedding if you live in a cold-weather climate.
- Complete change of clothing including a long sleeved shirt, long pants, extra socks and sturdy shoes. Consider additional clothing if you live in a cold-weather climate.
- Household chlorine bleach and medicine dropper. When diluted nine parts water to one part bleach, bleach can be used as a disinfectant. Or in an emergency, you can use it to treat water by using 16 drops of regular household liquid bleach per gallon of water. Do not use scented, color safe or bleaches with added cleaners.
- Fire Extinguisher
- Matches in a waterproof container and/or a magnesium fire starter.
- Feminine supplies and personal hygiene items.

- Mess kits, paper cups, plates and plastic utensils, and paper towels.
- Paper and pencil.
- Books, games, puzzles or other activities for children.
- Mp3 player (don't forget extra batteries!).

Household Chemicals:

- Nearly every household uses products containing hazardous materials or chemicals.
- It is critical to store household chemicals in places where children cannot access them. Remember that products such as aerosol cans of hair spray and deodorant, nail polish and nail polish remover, toilet bowl cleaners, and furniture polishes all fall into the category of hazardous materials.
- Buy only as much of a chemical as you think you will use. Leftover material can be shared with neighbors or donated to a business, charity, or government agency.
- Keep products containing hazardous materials in their original containers and never remove the labels unless the container is corroding. Corroding containers should be repackaged and clearly labeled.
- Never store hazardous products in food containers.
- Never mix household hazardous chemicals or waste with other products. Incompatibles, such as chlorine bleach and ammonia, may react, ignite, or explode.
- Follow the manufacturer's instructors for the proper use of the household chemical.
- Never smoke while using household chemicals.
- Never use hair spray, cleaning solutions, paint products, or pesticides near an open flame (e.g., pilot light, lighted candle, fireplace, wood burning stove, etc.) Although you may not be able to see or smell them, vapor particles in the air could catch fire or explode.
- Clean up any chemical spill immediately. Use rags to clean up the spill. Wear gloves and eye protection. Allow the fumes in the rags to evaporate outdoors. Dispose of the rags by wrapping

them in a newspaper and placing them in a sealed plastic bag in your trash can.

- Dispose of hazardous materials correctly. Take household hazardous waste to a local collection program. Check with your county or state ecological or solid waste agency to learn if there is a household hazardous waste collection program in your area.
- Post the number of the emergency medical services and the poison control center by all telephones or in your cell phone. In an emergency situation, you may not have time to look up critical phone numbers.

Earthquake:
Before the earthquake:
- Check for Hazards in the Home
  - o Fasten shelves securely to walls.
  - o Place large or heavy objects on lower shelves.
  - o Store breakable items such as bottled foods, glass, and china in low, closed cabinets with latches.
  - o Hang heavy items such as pictures and mirrors away from beds, couches, and anywhere people sit.
  - o Brace overhead light fixtures.
  - o Repair defective electrical wiring and leaky gas connections. These are potential fire risks.
  - o Secure a water heater by strapping it to the wall studs and bolting it to the floor.
  - o Repair any deep cracks in ceilings or foundations. Get expert advice if there are signs of structural defects.
  - o Store weed killers, pesticides, and flammable products securely in closed cabinets with latches and on bottom shelves.
- Identify Safe Places Indoors and Outdoors
  - o Under sturdy furniture such as a heavy desk or table.
  - o Against an inside wall.
  - o Away from areas where glass could shatter around windows, mirrors, pictures, or where heavy bookcases or other heavy furniture could fall over.

      o In the open, away from buildings, trees, and telephone and electrical lines, overpasses, or elevated expressways.

During the earthquake:

If indoors

- DROP to the ground; take COVER by getting under a sturdy table or other piece of furniture; and HOLD ON until the shaking stops. If there isn't a table or desk near you, cover your face and head with your arms and crouch in an inside corner of the building.
- Stay away from glass, windows, outside doors and walls, and anything that could fall, such as lighting fixtures or furniture.
- Stay in bed if you are there when the earthquake strikes. Hold on and protect your head with a pillow, unless you are under a heavy light fixture that could fall. In that case, move to the nearest safe place.
- Use a doorway for shelter only if it is near to you and if you know it is a strongly supported, loadbearing doorway.
- Stay inside until the shaking stops and it is safe to go outside. Research has shown that most injuries occur when people inside buildings attempt to move to a different location inside the building or try to leave.
- Be aware that the electricity may go out or the sprinkler systems or fire alarms may turn on.
- DO NOT use the elevators.

If outdoors

- Stay there.
- Move away from buildings, streetlights, and utility wires.
- Once in the open, stay there until the shaking stops. The greatest danger exists directly outside buildings, at exits and alongside exterior walls. Ground movement during an earthquake is seldom the direct cause of death or injury. Most earthquake-related casualties result from collapsing walls, flying glass, and falling objects.

If in a moving vehicle
- Stop as quickly as safety permits and stay in the vehicle. Avoid stopping near or under buildings, trees, overpasses, and utility wires.
- Proceed cautiously once the earthquake has stopped. Avoid roads, bridges, or ramps that might have been damaged by the earthquake.

If trapped under debris
- Do not light a match.
- Do not move about or kick up dust.
- Cover your mouth with a handkerchief or clothing.
- Tap on a pipe or wall so rescuers can locate you. Use a whistle if one is available. Shout only as a last resort. Shouting can cause you to inhale dangerous amounts of dust.

After the earthquake:
- Expect aftershocks. These secondary shockwaves are usually less violent than the main quake but can be strong enough to do additional damage to weakened structures. They can occur in the first hours, days, weeks, or even months after the quake.
- Listen to a battery-operated radio or television. Listen for the latest emergency information.
- Use the telephone only for emergency calls.
- Open cabinets cautiously. Beware of objects that can fall off shelves.
- Stay away from damaged areas. Stay away unless your assistance has been specifically requested by police, fire, or relief organizations. Return home only when authorities say it is safe.
- Be aware of possible tsunamis if you live in coastal areas. These are also known as seismic sea waves which are mistakenly called "tidal waves". When local authorities issue a tsunami warning, assume that a series of dangerous waves is on the way. Stay away from the beach. Move as far inland as you can.
- Help injured or trapped persons. Remember to help your neighbors who may require special assistance such as infants,

the elderly, and people with disabilities. Give first aid where appropriate. Do not move seriously injured persons unless they are in immediate danger of further injury. Call for help.

- Clean up spilled medicines, bleaches, gasoline or other flammable liquids immediately. Leave the area if you smell gas or fumes from other chemicals.
- Inspect the entire length of chimneys for damage. Unnoticed damage could lead to a fire.
- Inspect utilities.
    - o Check for gas leaks. If you smell gas or hear blowing or hissing noise, open a window and quickly leave the building. Turn off the gas at the outside main valve if you can and call the gas company from a neighbor's home. If you turn off the gas for any reason, it must be turned back on by a professional.
    - o Look for electrical system damage. If you see sparks or broken or frayed wires, or if you smell hot insulation, turn off the electricity at the main fuse box or circuit breaker. If you have to step in water to get to the fuse box or circuit breaker, call an electrician first for advice.
    - o Check for sewage and water lines damage. If you suspect sewage lines are damaged, avoid using the toilets and call a plumber. If water pipes are damaged, contact the water company and avoid using water from the tap. You can obtain safe water by melting ice cubes.

Fire or Wildfire:
To Prevent Fires:
Smoke Alarms
- Install smoke alarms. Properly working smoke alarms decrease your chances of dying in a fire by half.
- Place smoke alarms on every level of your residence. Place them outside bedrooms on the ceiling or high on the wall (4 to 12 inches from ceiling); at the top of open stairways; or at the bottom of enclosed stairs and near, but not in, the kitchen.
- Test and clean smoke alarms once a month and replace batteries at least once a year. Replace smoke alarms once every 10 years.

Escaping the Fire
- Review escape routes with your family. Practice escaping from each room.
- Make sure windows are not nailed or painted shut. Make sure security gratings on windows have a fire safety opening feature so they can be easily opened from the inside.
- Consider escape ladders if your residence has more than one level. Ensure that burglar bars and other antitheft mechanisms that block outside window entry are easily opened from the inside.
- Teach family members to stay low to the floor where the air is safer in a fire while escaping from a fire.

Flammable Items
- Never use gasoline, benzene, naphtha, or similar flammable liquids indoors.
- Store flammable liquids in approved containers in well-ventilated storage areas.
- Never smoke near flammable liquids.
- Discard all rags or materials that have been soaked in flammable liquids after you have used them. Safely discard them outdoors in a metal container.
- Insulate chimneys and place spark arresters on top. The chimney should be at least three feet higher than the roof. Remove branches hanging above and around the chimney.

Heating Sources
- Be careful when using alternative heating sources.
- Check with your local fire department on the legality of using kerosene heaters in your community. Be sure to fill kerosene heaters outside, and be sure they have cooled.
- Place heaters at least three feet away from flammable materials. Make sure the floor and nearby walls are properly insulated.
- Use only the type of fuel designated for your unit and follow manufacturer's instructions.

- Store ashes in a metal container outside and away from your residence.
- Keep open flames away from walls, furniture, drapery, and flammable items.
- Keep a screen in front of the fireplace.
- Have heating units inspected and cleaned annually by a certified specialist.

Matches and Smoking
- Keep matches and lighters up high, away from children, and, if possible, in a locked cabinet.
- Never smoke in bed or when drowsy or medicated. Provide smokers with deep, sturdy ashtrays. Douse cigarette and cigar butts with water before disposal.

Electrical Wiring
- If you have concerns, have the electrical wiring in your residence checked by an electrician.
- Inspect extension cords for frayed or exposed wires or loose plugs.
- Make sure outlets have cover plates and no exposed wiring.
- Make sure wiring does not run under rugs, over nails, or across high-traffic areas.
- Do not overload extension cords or outlets. If you need to plug in two or three appliances, get a UL-approved unit with built-in circuit breakers to prevent sparks and short circuits.
- Make sure insulation does not touch bare electrical wiring.

Other
- Sleep with your door closed.
- Install A-B-C-type fire extinguishers in your residence and teach family members how to use them.
- Consider installing an automatic fire sprinkler system in your residence.
- Ask your local fire department to inspect your residence for fire safety and prevention.

During and After a Fire:

If your clothes catch on fire, you should:
- Stop, drop, and roll - until the fire is extinguished. Running only makes the fire burn faster.

To escape a fire, you should:
- Check closed doors for heat before you open them. If you are escaping through a closed door, use the back of your hand to feel the top of the door, the doorknob, and the crack between the door and door frame before you open it. Never use the palm of your hand or fingers to test for heat - burning those areas could impair your ability to escape a fire.

Hot Door	Cool Door
Do not open. Escape through a window. If you cannot escape, hang a white or light-colored sheet outside the window, alerting fire fighters to your presence.	Open slowly and ensure fire and/or smoke is not blocking your escape route. If your escape route is blocked, shut the door immediately and use an alternate escape route, such as a window. If clear, leave immediately through the door and close it behind you. Be prepared to crawl. Smoke and heat rise. The air is clearer and cooler near the floor.

- Crawl low under any smoke to your exit - heavy smoke and poisonous gases collect first along the ceiling.
- Close doors behind you as you escape to delay the spread of the fire.
- Stay out once you are safely out. Do not reenter. Call 9-1-1.
- If you are with burn victims, or are a burn victim yourself, call 9-1-1; cool and cover burns to reduce chance of further injury or infection.
- If you detect heat or smoke when entering a damaged building, evacuate immediately.
- If you have a safe or strong box, do not try to open it. It can hold intense heat for several hours. If the door is opened before the box has cooled, the contents could burst into flames.

- If you must leave your home because a building inspector says the building is unsafe, ask someone you trust to watch the property during your absence.

Flood:

- Avoid building a home in a flood prone area unless you elevate and reinforce your home.
- Elevate the furnace, water heater, and electric panel if susceptible to flooding.
- Install "check valves" in sewer traps to prevent floodwater from backing up into the drains of your home.
- Contact community officials to find out if they are planning to construct barriers (levees, beams, floodwalls) to stop floodwater from entering the homes in your area.
- Seal the walls in your basement with waterproofing compounds to avoid seepage.
- Listen to the radio or television for information.
- Be aware that flash flooding can occur. If there is any possibility of a flash flood, move immediately to higher ground. Do not wait for instructions to move.
- Be aware of streams, drainage channels, canyons, and other areas known to flood suddenly. Flash floods can occur in these areas with or without such typical warnings as rain clouds or heavy rain.

If you must prepare to evacuate, you should do the following:

- Secure your home. If you have time, bring in outdoor furniture. Move essential items to an upper floor.
- Turn off utilities at the main switches or valves if instructed to do so. Disconnect electrical appliances. Do not touch electrical equipment if you are wet or standing in water.

If you have to leave your home, remember these evacuation tips:

- Do not walk through moving water. Six inches of moving water can make you fall. If you have to walk in water, walk where the water is not moving. Use a stick to check the firmness of the ground in front of you.

- Do not drive into flooded areas. If floodwaters rise around your car, abandon the car and move to higher ground if you can do so safely. You and the vehicle can be quickly swept away.

The following are important points to remember when driving in flood conditions:

- Six inches of water will reach the bottom of most passenger cars causing loss of control and possible stalling.
- A foot of water will float many vehicles.
- Two feet of rushing water can carry away most vehicles including sport utility vehicles (SUV's) and pick-ups.

After a flood:

- Listen for news reports to learn whether the community's water supply is safe to drink.
- Avoid floodwaters; water may be contaminated by oil, gasoline, or raw sewage. Water may also be electrically charged from underground or downed power lines.
- Avoid moving water.
- Be aware of areas where floodwaters have receded. Roads may have weakened and could collapse under the weight of a car.
- Stay away from downed power lines, and report them to the power company.
- Return home only when authorities indicate it is safe.
- Stay out of any building if it is surrounded by floodwaters.
- Use extreme caution when entering buildings; there may be hidden damage, particularly in foundations.
- Service damaged septic tanks, cesspools, pits, and leaching systems as soon as possible. Damaged sewage systems are serious health hazards.
- Clean and disinfect everything that got wet. Mud left from floodwater can contain sewage and chemicals.

Hurricane:

- Make plans to secure your property. Permanent storm shutters offer the best protection for windows. A second option is to board up windows with 5/8" marine plywood, cut to fit and ready to install.
- Tape does not prevent windows from breaking.
- Install straps or additional clips to securely fasten your roof to the frame structure. This will reduce roof damage.
- Be sure trees and shrubs around your home are well trimmed.
- Clear loose and clogged rain gutters and downspouts.
- Determine how and where to secure your boat.
- Consider building a safe room.

If a hurricane is likely in your area, you should:

- Listen to the radio or TV for information.
- Secure your home, close storm shutters, and secure outdoor objects or bring them indoors.
- Turn off utilities if instructed to do so. Otherwise, turn the refrigerator thermostat to its coldest setting and keep the doors closed.
- Turn off propane tanks.
- Avoid using the phone, except for serious emergencies.
- Secure your boat if time permits.
- Ensure a supply of water for sanitary purposes such as cleaning and flushing toilets. Fill the bathtub and other large containers with water.

You should evacuate under the following conditions:

- If you are directed by local authorities to do so. Be sure to follow their instructions.
- If you live in a mobile home or temporary structure—such shelters are particularly hazardous during hurricanes no matter how well fastened to the ground.
- If you live in a high-rise building—hurricane winds are stronger at higher elevations.
- If you live on the coast, on a floodplain, near a river, or on an inland waterway.
- If you feel you are in danger.

If you are unable to evacuate, go to your safe room. If you do not have one, follow these guidelines:

- Stay indoors during the hurricane and away from windows and glass doors.
- Close all interior doors—secure and brace external doors.
- Keep curtains and blinds closed. Do not be fooled if there is a lull; it could be the eye of the storm. Winds will pick up again.
- Take refuge in a small interior room, closet, or hallway on the lowest level.
- Lie on the floor under a table or another sturdy object.

Returning Home:

- When you go inside your home, there are certain things you should and should not do. Enter the home carefully and check for damage. Be aware of loose boards and slippery floors.
- Natural gas. If you smell gas or hear a hissing or blowing sound, open a window and leave immediately. Turn off the main gas valve from the outside, if you can. Call the gas company from a neighbor's residence. If you shut off the gas supply at the main valve, you will need a professional to turn it back on. Do not smoke or use oil, gas lanterns, candles, or torches for lighting inside a damaged home until you are sure there is no leaking gas or other flammable materials present.
- Sparks, broken or frayed wires. Check the electrical system unless you are wet, standing in water, or unsure of your safety. If possible, turn off the electricity at the main fuse box or circuit breaker. If the situation is unsafe, leave the building and call for help. Do not turn on the lights until you are sure they're safe to use. You may want to have an electrician inspect your wiring.
- Roof, foundation, and chimney cracks. If it looks like the building may collapse, leave immediately.
- Appliances. If appliances are wet, turn off the electricity at the main fuse box or circuit breaker. Then, unplug appliances and let them dry out. Have appliances checked by a professional before using them again. Also, have the electrical system checked by an electrician before turning the power back on.

- Water and sewage systems. If pipes are damaged, turn off the main water valve. Check with local authorities before using any water; the water could be contaminated. Pump out wells and have the water tested by authorities before drinking. Do not flush toilets until you know that sewage lines are in working condition.
- Food and other supplies. Throw out all food and other supplies that you suspect may have become contaminated or come in to contact with floodwater.
- Your basement. If your basement has flooded, pump it out gradually (about one third of the water per day) to avoid damage. The walls may collapse and the floor may buckle if the basement is pumped out while the surrounding ground is still waterlogged.
- Open cabinets. Be alert for objects that may fall.
- Clean up household chemical spills. Disinfect items that may have been contaminated by raw sewage, bacteria, or chemicals. Also clean salvageable items.
- **Call your insurance agent**. Take pictures of damages. Keep good records of repair and cleaning costs.

Thunderstorm:

- Remove dead or rotting trees and branches that could fall and cause injury or damage during a severe thunderstorm.
- It is very important that you get out of the way of a storm approaching, if possible.
- Always make sure to stay inside until the storm has completely passed. There should be at least 30 minutes pass after the last clasp of thunder.
- Stay away from windows in the event there is flying debris or lightning.
- When there is lightning, make sure to unplug major appliances and turn off air conditioners to avoid a power surge in the event of a power failure.
- Avoid showering or bathing. Plumbing and bathroom fixtures can conduct electricity.

- If you see someone outside on the ground and suspect they are victim of a lightning strike and call 9–1–1 immediately.

Tornado:
Facts:
- They may strike quickly, with little or no warning.
- They may appear nearly transparent until dust and debris are picked up or a cloud forms in the funnel.
- The average tornado moves Southwest to Northeast, but many tornadoes have been known to move in any direction.
- The average forward speed of a tornado is 30 MPH, but may vary from stationary to 70 MPH.
- Tornadoes can accompany tropical storms and hurricanes as they move onto land.
- Waterspouts are tornadoes that form over water.
- Tornadoes are most frequently reported east of the Rocky Mountains during spring and summer months.
- Peak tornado season in the southern states is March through May; in the northern states, it is late spring through early summer.
- Tornadoes are most likely to occur between 3 p.m. and 9 p.m., but can occur at any time.
- Look for the following danger signs:
  o Dark, often greenish sky
  o Large hail
  o A large, dark, low-lying cloud (particularly if rotating)
  o Loud roar, similar to a freight train.

During a Tornado:

If you are under a tornado WARNING, seek shelter immediately.

If You Are:	Then:
In a structure (e.g. residence, small building, school, nursing home, hospital, factory, shopping center, high-rise building)	Go to a pre-designated shelter area such as a safe room, basement, storm cellar, or the lowest building level. If there is no basement, go to the center of an interior room on the lowest level (closet, interior hallway) away from corners, windows, doors, and outside walls. Put as many walls as possible between you and the outside. Get under a sturdy table and use your arms to protect your head and neck. Do not open windows.

If You Are:	Then:
In a vehicle, trailer, or mobile home	Get out immediately and go to the lowest floor of a sturdy, nearby building or a storm shelter. Mobile homes, even if tied down, offer little protection from tornadoes.
Outside with no shelter	Lie flat in a nearby ditch or depression and cover your head with your hands. Be aware of the potential for flooding. Do not get under an overpass or bridge. You are safer in a low, flat location. Never try to outrun a tornado in urban or congested areas in a car or truck. Instead, leave the vehicle immediately for safe shelter. Watch out for flying debris. Flying debris from tornadoes causes most fatalities and injuries.

After a tornado:

- When you go inside your home, there are certain things you should and should not do. Enter the home carefully and check for damage. Be aware of loose boards and slippery floors.
- Natural gas. If you smell gas or hear a hissing or blowing sound, open a window and leave immediately. Turn off the main gas valve from the outside, if you can. Call the gas company from a neighbor's residence. If you shut off the gas supply at the main valve, you will need a professional to turn it back on. Do not smoke or use oil, gas lanterns, candles, or torches for lighting inside a damaged home until you are sure there is no leaking gas or other flammable materials present.
- Sparks, broken or frayed wires. Check the electrical system unless you are wet, standing in water, or unsure of your safety. If possible, turn off the electricity at the main fuse box or circuit breaker. If the situation is unsafe, leave the building and call for help. Do not turn on the lights until you are sure they're safe to use. You may want to have an electrician inspect your wiring.
- Roof, foundation, and chimney cracks. If it looks like the building may collapse, leave immediately.

- Appliances. If appliances are wet, turn off the electricity at the main fuse box or circuit breaker. Then, unplug appliances and let them dry out. Have appliances checked by a professional before using them again. Also, have the electrical system checked by an electrician before turning the power back on.
- Water and sewage systems. If pipes are damaged, turn off the main water valve. Check with local authorities before using any water; the water could be contaminated. Pump out wells and have the water tested by authorities before drinking. Do not flush toilets until you know that sewage lines are in working condition.
- Food and other supplies. Throw out all food and other supplies that you suspect may have become contaminated or come in to contact with floodwater.
- Your basement. If your basement has flooded, pump it out gradually (about one third of the water per day) to avoid damage. The walls may collapse and the floor may buckle if the basement is pumped out while the surrounding ground is still waterlogged.
- Open cabinets. Be alert for objects that may fall.
- Clean up household chemical spills. Disinfect items that may have been contaminated by raw sewage, bacteria, or chemicals. Also clean salvageable items.
- Call your insurance agent. Take pictures of damages. Keep good records of repair and cleaning costs.

Winter Storm:
Add the following supplies to your disaster supplies kit:
- Rock salt to melt ice on walkways.
- Sand to improve traction.
- Snow shovels and other snow removal equipment.

Prepare your home and family
- Prepare for possible isolation in your home by having sufficient heating fuel; regular fuel sources may be cut off. For example, store a good supply of dry, seasoned wood for your fireplace or wood-burning stove.

- Winterize your home to extend the life of your fuel supply by insulating walls and attics, caulking and weather-stripping doors and windows, and installing storm windows or covering windows with plastic.
- Winterize your barn, shed or any other structure that may provide shelter for your family, neighbors, livestock or equipment. Clear rain gutters; repair roof leaks and cut away tree branches that could fall on a house or other structure during a storm.
- Insulate pipes with insulation or newspapers and plastic and allow faucets to drip a little during cold weather to avoid freezing.
- Keep fire extinguishers on hand, and make sure everyone in your home knows how to use them. House fires pose an additional risk, as more people turn to alternate heating sources without taking the necessary safety precautions.
- Learn how to shut off water valves in case a pipe bursts.
- Know ahead of time what you should do to help elderly or disabled friends, neighbors or employees.
- Hire a contractor to check the structural ability of the roof to sustain unusually heavy weight from the accumulation of snow or water, if drains on flat roofs do not work.

Prepare your car
- Check or have a mechanic check the following items on your car:
  - o Antifreeze levels - ensure they are sufficient to avoid freezing.
  - o Battery and ignition system - should be in top condition and battery terminals should be clean.
  - o Brakes - check for wear and fluid levels.
  - o Exhaust system - check for leaks and crimped pipes and repair or replace as necessary. Carbon monoxide is deadly and usually gives no warning.
  - o Fuel and air filters - replace and keep water out of the system by using additives and maintaining a full tank of gas.
  - o Heater and defroster - ensure they work properly.
  - o Lights and flashing hazard lights - check fuses and bulbs.

- o Oil - check for level and weight. Heavier oils thicken more at low temperatures and do not lubricate as well.
  - o Thermostat - ensure it works properly.
  - o Windshield wiper equipment – Make sure to repair any problems and maintain proper washer fluid level.
- Install good winter tires. Make sure the tires have adequate tread. All-weather radials are usually adequate for most winter conditions. However, some jurisdictions require that to drive on their roads. Vehicles must be equipped with chains or snow tires with studs.
- Maintain at least a half tank of gas at all times during the winter season.
- Place a winter emergency kit in each car that includes:
  - o a shovel
  - o windshield scraper and small broom
  - o flashlight
  - o battery powered radio
  - o extra batteries
  - o water
  - o snack food
  - o matches
  - o extra hats, socks and mittens
  - o first aid kit with pocket knife
  - o necessary medications
  - o blanket(s)
  - o tow chain or rope
  - o road salt and sand
  - o booster cables
  - o emergency flares
  - o fluorescent distress flag

Dress for the Weather
- Wear several layers of loose fitting, light-weight warm clothing rather than one layer of heavy clothing. The outer garments should be tightly woven and water repellent.
- Wear mittens, which are warmer than gloves.

- Wear a hat.
- Cover your mouth with a scarf to protect your lungs.

During the winter storm:
- Listen to your radio, television, or NOAA Weather Radio for weather reports and emergency information.
- Eat regularly and drink ample fluids, but avoid caffeine and alcohol.
- Conserve fuel, if necessary, by keeping your residence cooler than normal. Temporarily close off heat to some rooms.
- If the pipes freeze, remove any insulation or layers of newspapers and wrap pipes in rags. Completely open all faucets and pour hot water over the pipes, starting where they were most exposed to the cold or where the cold was most likely to penetrate.
- Maintain ventilation when using kerosene heaters to avoid buildup of toxic fumes. Refuel kerosene heaters outside and keep them at least three feet from flammable objects.

If you are outdoors
- Avoid overexertion when shoveling snow. Overexertion can bring on a heart attack—a major cause of death in the winter. If you must shovel snow, stretch before going outside.
- Cover your mouth. Protect your lungs from extremely cold air by covering your mouth when outdoors. Try not to speak unless absolutely necessary.
- Keep dry. Change wet clothing frequently to prevent a loss of body heat. Wet clothing loses all of its insulating value and transmits heat rapidly.
- Watch for signs of frostbite. These include loss of feeling and white or pale appearance in extremities such as fingers, toes, ear lobes, and the tip of the nose. If symptoms are detected, get medical help immediately.
- Watch for signs of hypothermia. These include uncontrollable shivering, memory loss, disorientation, incoherence, slurred speech, drowsiness, and apparent exhaustion.
- If symptoms of hypothermia are detected:

o Get the victim to a warm location.

o Remove wet clothing.

o Put the person in dry clothing and wrap their entire body in a blanket;

o Warm the center of the body first.

o Give warm, non-alcoholic or non-caffeinated beverages if the victim is conscious.

o Get medical help as soon as possible.

If you are driving

- Drive only if it is necessary. If you must drive, consider the following:

  o Travel in the day, don't travel alone, and keep others informed of your schedule.

  o Stay on main roads; avoid back road shortcuts.

If a blizzard traps you in the car:

o Pull off the highway. Turn on hazard lights and hang a distress flag from the radio antenna or window.

o Remain in your vehicle where rescuers are most likely to find you. Do not set out on foot unless you can see a building close by where you know you can take shelter. Be careful; distances are distorted by blowing snow. A building may seem close, but be too far to walk to in deep snow.

o Run the engine and heater about 10 minutes each hour to keep warm. When the engine is running, open a downwind window slightly for ventilation and periodically clear snow from the exhaust pipe. This will protect you from possible carbon monoxide poisoning.

o Exercise to maintain body heat, but avoid overexertion. In extreme cold, use road maps, seat covers, and floor mats for insulation. Huddle with passengers and use your coat for a blanket.

o Take turns sleeping. One person should be awake at all times to look for rescue crews.

o Drink fluids to avoid dehydration.

o Be careful not to waste battery power. Balance electrical energy needs - the use of lights, heat, and radio - with supply.

o Turn on the inside light at night so work crews or rescuers can see you.

o If stranded in a remote area, stomp large block letters in an open area spelling out HELP or SOS and line with rocks or tree limbs to attract the attention of rescue personnel who may be surveying the area by airplane.

o Leave the car and proceed on foot - if necessary - once the blizzard passes.

After the winter storm:

- Remove and discard items that cannot be washed and disinfected.
- Stay away from damaged buildings or structures that have not been examined and certified by an inspector.
- Wear hard hats, goggles, heavy work gloves, and watertight boots with steel toe and insole (not just steel shank) for cleanup work.
- Wear earplugs or protective headphones to reduce risk from equipment noise.
- When using a chain saw, operate the saw according to the manufacturer's instructions, wear appropriate protective equipment, avoid contact with power lines, be sure that bystanders are at a safe distance, and take extra care in cutting trees or branches that have gotten bent or caught under another object. Use extreme caution to avoid electrical shock when using an electric chainsaw.
- **Call your insurance agent.** Take pictures of damages. Keep good records of repair and cleaning costs.

Chapter 28

"Boomerang Kids"

While most young adults feel ready to move out on their own, reality sets in shortly after they leave their parents' home. There are some circumstances that cannot be avoided such as graduated college and can't find employment, loss of job, economics or illness that may require you to move back home. I know that it can create a hardship on both parties, but if you both work together, it doesn't have to be a devastating experience on either end. Do not always expect your parents to bail you out when times are rough. Stand up to your responsibilities.

Definition:
- Young adults in western culture so named for the frequency with which they choose to cohabitate with their parents after a brief period of living on their own–thus returning or "boomeranging" back to their original home. This cohabitation can take many forms, ranging from situations that mirror the high dependency of pre-adulthood to highly independent, separate-household arrangements.
- The term is most meaningful applied to those in middle-class.

On the Positive side:
- Takes financial relief off the young adult. It will allow them to regroup and learn those skills that they were lacking when they left the first time.

- Working parents have more help with young siblings and/or household chores.
- This can benefit parents when they reach old age. In societies where it is common for children to live with their parents into adulthood, such as Asian, and Hispanic cultures, children more frequently take care of aging parents, rather than transferring the responsibility to a third party, such as a nursing home.

On the Negative side:

- Financial and social independence of the young adult may be lost.
- May cause a financial burden on the parents.
- "Empty nesters" may now consider themselves as "crowded nesters."
- Young adults who are able to return home after an unsuccessful job hunt may become more passive in their search for employment if they continue to be financially supported by their parents.
- A lack of motivation can possibly delay the start to a young adult's career and cause him/her to miss months or years of job earnings and experience.
- Where living space is shared, gatherings with friends can be limited in frequency or scope.
- Dating is similarly constrained and can be impaired by the stigma of the young adult's perceived inability to function independent of his/her parents.

Next Steps:

You both must agree on the following steps to make this work.

- Have "the" discussion early on to ensure that everyone has the same expectations about the living arrangement. Define why you are moving back home: to start a career and save money, prepare for more schooling or take a break from everything.
- Set clear expectations by talking about obligations regarding expenses and household chores. Discuss whether dates over

for dinner or even to spend the night are acceptable. By setting and enforcing expectations, your parents will help you learn the skills you need to live independently.

- Set a time limit. If your ultimate goal is independence, there has to be a time limit set for how long you can live in their house. Experts say it's best for everyone to be working with the same understanding to avoid the resentment that might arise from unspecified assumptions.
- Pay Rent. For some parents, it will be difficult to charge rent to family. But for other parents, charging rent, even a minimal amount, helps prepare you for living independently and helps parents keep up with home finances. For parents: If you choose, you can set aside that rent for a down payment to assist them when they are ready to move out on their own.
- Hold to agreements. If you hold to the agreements and continue to respect one another, there shouldn't be many problems. Resentment can arise when either parents or children are not doing what they've agreed upon. Keep up the expectations and boundaries.

Chapter 29

Making Funeral Arrangements

This section is not only for making the arrangements for others, but also for making sure that your own wishes are met in the event of your passing. No one looks forward to making funeral arrangements; however, it is an unfortunate part of life. Planning the memorial service does not have to be difficult. The key is to handle one task at a time and solicit help from your family and friends. There are different options available, and no two funerals are the same. Make sure to spell out your wishes in your Last Will and Testament so that your family knows what you want.

Benefits of Planning Ahead:
- It makes your wishes known ahead of time.
- Family can be involved in making these difficult decisions.
- It relieves your loved ones of the financial obligation.
- Have a last will and testament created. Update it as your life situation changes.
- Have a living will created. A living will is a legal document that a person uses to make his or her wishes known regarding life-prolonging medical treatments in the event they are not conscious to do so themselves. This is also known as an advanced directive.

- Planning ahead ensures that your family and funeral director know exactly what kind of funeral you want. Families tend to take comfort at the time of death, simply from knowing their loved one's funeral reflects his or her wishes.

Planning ahead may or may not involve prepaying. Prepaying for a funeral offers you the advantage of paying for your funeral when you can afford it, thus relieving your family of a financial burden later. There are generally three basic ways to prepay for a funeral.

1. You can purchase an insurance policy that provides benefits equal to your funeral expenses.
2. You can enter into a trust fund agreement, depositing a specific amount of money in one lump sum or installments. The fund, managed by a trustee (such as a banker), is used to pay for funeral services and merchandise.
3. You can open a savings or certificate-of-deposit account earmarked for funeral expenses that would be payable upon death to the funeral home.

Most Services Provided by Funeral Directors:
- Transport of the deceased person's body to the funeral home.
- Securing of information for and filing of the certificate of death.
- Meeting with your family to discuss arrangement options.
- Helping you choose the place, type, and time for the visitation, service, and other arrangements.
- Helping you select a casket, outer burial container, urn, memorial stone, marker, or other items.
- Advising you about other decisions to make, such as choosing pallbearers and arranging for flowers.
- Helping with necessary paperwork, including obituary notices and a variety of government benefit claim forms.
- Helping you notify the deceased person's employer, attorney, insurance companies, and banks.
- Arranging for aftercare services to help you through the grieving process.

Not all of these services may be available, so check with your local funeral home on what they provide.

Types of Final Resting Options

- Earth burial is the most common form of final resting in the United States. Americans seem to prefer the idea of a final resting place and a gravesite where they can go to visit and remember the person who passed.
- Entombment offers a fixed final resting place. When a body is entombed, the casket is placed in a mausoleum, an above ground structure usually made of marble or stone. Mausoleums vary greatly in size and design and are often found on cemetery grounds. Some are large enough for entire families, with a separate room for each person's casket.
- Cremation is often accompanied by the rites (ceremonious acts) and ceremonies of the funeral, including embalming and visitation. Final resting options include earth burial, entombment, and scattering. Some families keep the cremated remains in an urn or other appropriate container for a period of time before deciding on a final resting place.
- Direct disposition is the immediate cremation or immediate burial of the body with no attendant rites or ceremonies.

No matter how the body is committed, most families choose some form of marker or monument to memorialize the deceased. Markers vary from large granite or marble memorials (with or without photos), to small bronze plaques placed over a grave. Many families who choose cremation and scatter the remains purchase space in a cemetery for a memorial plaque.

Making the Arrangements:

- Carry out the intended wishes of the deceased, whether you agree with them or not.
- Pick a funeral home. Choosing the funeral home is one of the easier tasks in funeral arrangement. However, family members need to speak with the director and discuss the procedure and cost. The director can also assist with coffins and burial plots.

- Choose a funeral location. Family members can plan to hold the memorial service at the funeral home or a church. If the deceased individual was not affiliated with a religious organization, a funeral home is a great location for the service.
- Select the casket or other final resting option.
- Select the casket spray colors and flowers.
- Decide if you want an open or closed casket.
- Arrange for military honors or honor guard, if applicable.
- Set a date and time for the memorial service. Speak with the funeral home and church and coordinate the date and time.
- Schedule a date for the wake. On average, relatives hold a wake or viewing one to two nights prior to the funeral services. This allows ample time for loved ones to view the body and comfort the deceased person's family.
- Post the obituary in the local paper and/or online. You can e-mail the link to family and friends. Many funeral homes offer a special Web page for this.
- Arrange for someone to house-sit during the visitation and funeral. Many home break-ins take place during this time because it is assumed that you will be out of the home during the days/hours posted in the obituary.
- Get hotel suggestions for out-of-town guests. List the information in your e-mail or online Web page.
- Plan the music and funeral program. While funerals are cheerless occasions, it is normal to choose music (organ music, prerecorded music, and singer) and develop a program of events.
- Select the scriptures and verses that you want read.
- Select a family member, clergy member, close friend, or business associate to provide the eulogy. This is a special time to highlight the deceased person's life, contributions, commendations, and lightly humorous personal stories.
- Select the pallbearers and honorary pallbearers.
- Pick out the clothing/dress articles for the deceased.
- Gather items for a memory board or memory table such as favorite pictures, memorabilia, etc., to be displayed during visitation.

- Coordinate an after-service meal. After a funeral service, it is customary for attendees to enjoy a meal together. Host the meal at a restaurant, a family member's home, or church hall, or use the funeral home's reception room.
- Make arrangements for your home cleaning and yard maintenance before and after the service—one less thing to worry about.

Post Funeral:

- Allow yourself to grieve.
- There are five stages to the grieving process (denial, anger, bargaining, depression, and acceptance), and each person deals with these stages differently; there is no time limit.
- Send thank-you cards for flowers, gifts, and food you received.
- Return dishes from food you received.
- Discuss your feelings with family and friends; do not keep everything bottled up inside.
- Do not be embarrassed to seek professional help for your grieving process.
- Do not take medications prescribed for other people to help you cope with grief; call your physician and get your own medication.
- Seek out a bereavement group to share with those who are feeling the same emotions as you.
- Accept help from others, no matter how big or small the offer.
- Arrange the reading of the will.
- Have the tombstone engraved and placed.
- Return borrowed items and any medical items that were left in the home.
- Obtain copies of the death certificate.
- Meet with the deceased's attorney to discuss the necessary legal processes.
- Notify the insurance companies and file all claims.
- Apply for the appropriate social security benefits, veteran benefits, and/or pension benefits.
- Notify your accountant or tax preparer.

- Notify the deceased's stockbroker, if applicable.
- Notify the deceased's bank.
- Notify the deceased's mortgage company, if applicable.
- Notify the department of motor vehicles to transfer titles.
- Notify the credit card companies.
- Notify any other loan companies.

Conclusion:
Other Important Things

Well, this is it for now. There are just a few more important items below for you to remember. I hope that this book has helped you or at least taught you something new. You should try to learn something new every day. Be thankful for each day that you spend on this earth and treat everyone as if it were your last day. Family and friends are a gift, so treat them as such. Work is only work if you do not like what you are doing. If work is your passion, you will never work a day in your life. There is a World Wide Web out there with demos on how to accomplish most of this advice, so take full advantage of it. Lastly, if someone gives you advice, at least listen. They are speaking from past life experience, which could be very valuable to you some day.

Last but Not Least:
- Tell everyone you love them daily!
- Follow your passion. Do what you love to do.
- Keep your sense of humor! Don't take everything in life so seriously. Life is 10% what happens to you and 90% how you respond to it.
- Call Mom/Dad (and other important family members) once a week.
- Make a calendar of all family birthdays or put them in your cal-

endar on your phone. You do not always have to send a gift. A call is sometimes the best gift you can give.

- Make sure everything is in off position before leaving the house.
- If you do not use something within nine months and can do without it, get rid of it. Do not be a packrat.
- Donate things to charity and get a receipt for tax purposes.
- Clean out under sinks (bathroom and kitchen) every six months, checking expiration dates.
- Get your mail every day. Open it and sort it. Put all bills in one place in date due order.
- Never leave candles burning unattended.
- Turn fans off when not in use.
- Recycle and help save our planet.
- *Do not* drink and drive.
- *Do not* text and drive.
- Limit cell phone calls while driving. Pull over in a safe place if you need to talk on the phone. Make sure you keep your car doors locked.
- If you must talk on the phone while driving (which I do not encourage), use a hands-free device. Just remember you are not fully focused on the road.
- Keep a flashlight or candles/matches in rooms without windows in the event of a power outage.
- Keep a flashlight in your car.
- If you have plastic or silk plants/flowers, dust them often with a damp cloth.
- If you have real plants/flowers, clean up after them often. Do not leave dead branches/leaves on the floor, as it may attract ants.
- If you have pets, remember that Poinsettias, Mistletoe, and Holly Berries are toxic to them.
- When you walk to your car in a parking garage, always carry your keys and make sure you are alert to what is going on around you.
- Never sit in your car in a parking lot or garage. Once you are inside the car, lock the doors, start the car, and leave.

- If you have a water softener system (water filtration system) outside, keep it filled with salt pellets. Check it at least every two weeks.
- Know what is going on in the world. Watch/listen or read the news daily.
- Know where your children are at all times. Communicate often. Do not assume someone else is watching them for you.
- Teach your children about stranger danger. There are too many missing children in the world today.
- Keep children away from pools. Install a gate and keep it locked at all times. Speak with neighbors to make sure they do the same. Prevent drowning.
- When time permits, volunteer at a food bank or local homeless kitchen. Be thankful for what you have.
- Never put off today what you could have done right now. Would it really take that long to do?
- Remember: "Success" is a process of continually seeking answers to new questions.
- Always put your faith in the Lord and he will help you overcome any hardship.

Resources

Twelve Time Management Habits by Benjamin Franklin, one of the Founding Fathers of the United States [World Wide Web]

Sixteen Rules for Investment Success (and for your family, house, tuition, retirement...). (1993). Core investment principles [Brochure]. Templeton, Sir John; Franklin Templeton Investments

Websites

www.about.com – This website has a wealth of information on home repairs, car care, appliance repair, plumbing, resume building and other interesting facts.

www.cancer.org – This website provides content on smoking and cardiovascular related issues.

www.ehow.com – This website contains information for General Home Repair and Car Maintenance suggestions. It is a detailed website however it states that the self-contributions to this website may or may not be correct depending on the subject matter. The content utilized in this book has been verified by a professional in that area.

www.fda.gov/food - This website contains lots of information on food handling, food storage, food spoilage and other food related issues.

www.fema.gov – This website contains information on Disaster Preparedness.

www.mypyramid.gov – This website has all of the information on how to read, understand and use the food pyramids.

www.youtube.com – This website contains "hands on" video demos for many of the instructional items in this book. For example: Sewing. There are many videos on the different types of stitches listed in this book.

Index

About the Author

MICHELE SFAKIANOS (*Sfa-can-iss*) is a Registered Nurse, Leading Authority on Life Skills, Speaker and Award Winning Author. In 1982, she received her **AS Degree in Business Data Processing/Computer Programming**. In 1993, she received her **Associate in Science degree in Nursing** from St. Petersburg Junior College, graduating with Honors. In 1999, Michele received her **Bachelor of Science degree in Nursing** from Florida International University, graduating with High Honors. Michele is also the owner of Open Pages Publishing, LLC offering quality self-publishing. Her first book *Useful Information for Everyday Living* was published October 2010 and was later changed to *The 4–1–1 on Life Skills* and released June 2011. Her other books include: *The 4–1–1 on Step Parenting*, released October 2011; *The 4–1–1 on Surviving Teenhood*, released October 2012; *Parenting with an Edge*, released June 2013; and *Teen Success: It's All About You! Your Choices – Your Life*, released June 2013. She is well respected in her areas of expertise. Her years of experience as a Registered Nurse, Mother, and Leading Authority on Parenting and Life Skills, have given her the knowledge and wisdom to write her books.

www.ingramcontent.com/pod-product-compliance
Lightning Source LLC
LaVergne TN
LVHW051517080426
835509LV00017B/2089